RACING MOTOR CYCLES

RACING
MOTOR
CYCLES

MICK WOOLLETT

Hamlyn
London New York Sydney Toronto

Published by the Hamlyn Publishing Group Limited
London · New York · Sydney · Toronto
Hamlyn House, Feltham, Middlesex, England
Copyright © The Hamlyn Publishing Group Limited 1973

ISBN 0 600 37544 7

Printed in England by Sir Joseph Causton and Sons Limited

CONTENTS

The majority of the photographs in this book were taken by the author, Mick Woollett. For additional illustrations the publishers are grateful to: Associated Press; Wolfgang Gruber; Keystone; Corrado Millanta; the Editor of *Motor Cycle*; Publifoto; Wolfgang Segel; Ulrich Schwab; R. J. Traynor. The paintings on pages 7, 11 and 15 are by Michael Turner.

THE FIRST CHAMPIONSHIPS

The Isle of Man Tourist Trophy was first run in 1907, but Grand Prix motorcycle racing really became established in the 1920s. During that decade such famous events as the Belgian, Italian, Ulster and German Grands Prix were held for the first time, and the Dutch TT was first run.

In the 1920s the races were long and punishing. The circuits consisted of normal roads which were closed for meetings, practice and the race. These were anything up to 20 miles to a lap and the surfaces were often rolled stones on a clay base – it was not until the 1930s that tar surfaces became universal.

The 500cc class was the major event at meetings and it was usually supported by 250cc and 350cc races. But there were so few competitors that all three classes usually raced together, each capacity group starting at intervals of a minute or so. Race distances were usually between 200 and 300 miles and some grands prix lasted over five hours!

It was a sport for iron men riding rugged and reliable bikes – men such as Graham Walker, Stanley Woods, Alec Bennett, Charlie Dodson, Wal Handley and Jimmy Simpson, on Norton, Rudge, Sunbeam, Velocette and AJS machines.

As speeds went up and the popularity of the sport grew so the organisation of the meetings took on a more professional air. To give the spectators more exciting programmes race distances were cut. This meant that the various capacity classes could be run as separate races – and this in turn allowed the star riders to compete in more than one race at a meeting, although few did so until after the war. Grand Prix racing as we know it today was taking shape and by the 1930s virtually every major nation of Western Europe had its Grand Prix, and a round of classic events had been established.

The riders often used to travel by rail – bikes and tool boxes were loaded into baggage vans while riders and mechanics settled down in comfort. So comprehensive was the rail system of Europe that the travelling times compared very favourably with those by road today.

One of the problems was transport from the station nearest to the circuit to the track itself. Nortons overcame this by virtually detailing their local agent to make the necessary arrangements – and such was the prestige of the famous British factory in the 1930s that most were delighted to help.

Norton in fact swept the board in both the 350 and the 500cc classes of Grand Prix racing through the early and mid-1930s, establishing a dominance that is only now being equalled by MV Agusta. But strangely enough there was no championship series. Each big race was an individual affair with no season-long championship theme to link them together.

The pre-war era of Norton supremacy came to an abrupt and tragic end when their famous Scottish star Jimmy Guthrie was killed in the 1937 German Grand Prix. He was leading the race, held at the Sachsenring, which is now the home of the East German Grand Prix, when he crashed on the last lap. At first it was reported that he had been forced off the road by a rider he was lapping, but it seems the real reason for his accident was a broken con rod that locked the engine.

He was mourned throughout Europe, and is still remembered by veteran racing enthusiasts. During the period from 1934 until his death in 1937 he had dominated the Grand Prix scene and once won the 500cc class of nine Continental Grands Prix in succession – a feat only beaten by Giacomo Agostini.

It was not that Norton lacked star riders after Guthrie's death. The fact is that this coincided with the rise of BMW. The German factory had been developing a supercharged flat-twin 500cc

Sidecar racing has always been spectacular! This moment from the Belgian Grand Prix of 1947 shows Belgian Marcel Masuy (BMW) battling to stay ahead of his compatriot Puttemans (Sarolea).

Opposite, top: this classic picture from the 1920s captures the atmosphere of those far away days. Taken at the Dutch TT in 1928 it shows AJS rider Charlie Hough crashing after colliding with Martinelli of Switzerland (Motosacoche).
Opposite, bottom: typical scene from the 1930s as Norton ace Jimmy Guthrie leads BMW teamsters Karl Gall and Otto Ley during the 500cc class of the Dutch TT.
Above: sunshine and straw-hats at a Belgian Grand Prix in the early 1920s. The road surface is rolled stones and clay and the machines are formed up in capacity groups because in those days all the races were run concurrently.
Below, right: most famous BMW rider of the pre-war era was Germany's Georg Meier here seen winning the 1939 Senior TT.

racer which in 1937 began to challenge the single cylinder Norton. The British machine had a very definite edge on road holding, and on the tricky circuits of the day this was enough to give them the advantage that year.

The Germans, helped by the Nazi government who were anxious to impress the world with sporting victories, were also challenging in the 250 and 350cc classes where teams on beautifully engineered DKW two-strokes were pressing their rivals hard.

It was at this period of change, the winter of 1937–38, that the first mutterings about a championship were heard. In Britain no one took much notice and the decision of the FICM (the international governing body of motor-cycle sport, now known as the FIM) to introduce a

European Championship for the 1938 season was to all intents and purpose ignored.

That year the titles were based on the results of the eight most important European races: the Isle of Man and Dutch TTs, and the Belgian, Swiss, French, German, Ulster and Italian Grands Prix. By this time BMW had made considerable progress towards solving their handling problems, and Georg Meier won the 500cc title for the German company. Harold Daniell, the tubby little Londoner who could not see without his glasses, won the Senior TT and finished a close second in the table with 16 points to Meier's 20.

Above: leading riders after the 1938 Senior TT — Stanley Woods (second), Harold Daniell (first) and Freddie Frith (third).
Below: the team that beat the BMWs in 1939 — Italian Dorino Serafini and the 500cc supercharged Gilera four.

Typical pre-war style as Germany's Ewald Kluge hustles his supercharged factory DKW to victory in the 1938 250cc Lightweight TT. Kluge was twice European champion.

In the 350cc class the DKWs failed. The championship was won by Ted Mellors on a Velocette. Mellors was one of the top professionals of the 1930s and although not a works rider in the accepted sense he won a total of 20 major races in the decade before the war.

However DKW did triumph in the 250cc class, where Ewald Kluge won all the major races and earned himself the title of Champion of the Year by scoring more points than any other rider irrespective of class. The first truly international motor-cycle road racing championship had been established and although few people took much notice of it at the time, the ball was rolling.

The Italians stepped in to challenge the Germans in 1939, while Norton, who had almost played a lone hand for Britain since the slump of the early 1930s had decimated the motor-cycle industry, pulled out. They realised that their unsupercharged single-cylinder machines had no chance against the blown multis, and in any case they were at full stretch with a massive military contract for their side-valve 490cc 16H model.

In the 500cc class the four-cylinder Italian Gilera which sported water-cooling and a super-charger was more than a match for the BMW, and when it kept going nothing on two wheels could catch it. The championship series of nine races (the Swedish GP had been added) was cut to seven by the outbreak of the Second World War, but the FICM awarded the titles. Gilera's number one, Dorino Serafini, was the new 500cc champion with 23 points, five more than Meier.

Mellors again took the 350cc title on his Velocette but only by the very narrowest margin. In fact he tied on points with DKW ace Heiner Fleischmann but gained the title because he had finished ahead of the German in the Belgian Grand Prix which was the Grand Prix of Europe that year. Between the wars this title circulated among the classics and was supposed to be the most important race of the year. At least it made a good tie-breaker for the championships.

Little Kluge again won the 250cc title and came out tops in the overall championship but by the time the results were announced most people had other things to think about as war rolled over Europe. It was the end of international motor-cycle racing for over six years, and the end of the old European championship system.

POST-WAR REVIVAL

Most of the great names of racing survived the war and so did many of the machines that had been making history in 1939. But until the 1951 season there was, to use a contemporary expression, 'no fraternization' in motor-cycle sport between the allied nations and the Germans.

This was understandable. The memories of a bitterly fought war were too fresh to allow an immediate resumption of sporting activities. So although Georg Meier was soon back racing a supercharged BMW in his native Germany and Harold Daniell started again where he had left off in 1939, on a factory Norton, they never again clashed on a circuit, for both had retired by 1951.

The Italians had escaped the wrath that barred the Germans. They had committed none of the mass atrocities of the Nazis and had in any case changed sides and joined the Allies towards the end of the war. So when racing resumed in 1946 and 1947 they were free to join in.

Those were difficult days. Many things were rationed throughout most of Europe. Petrol had an octane rating of 72 and was more akin to top grade heating oil than racing fuel. New machines were scarce as gold as the factories strove to switch from the production of military equipment to peace-time goods. And the demand for any sort of transport was so great that few had time even to think about racing, let alone design and produce new bikes.

It was during this period of re-adjustment from war to peace that the Fédération Internationale des Clubs Motocyclistes made some far-reaching decisions. Meeting in London in December 1946 the delegates decided on two major steps.

First, it was decided to confine fuel to normally available pump grades (in pre-war days up to 50 per cent of Benzole had been allowed, which effectively raised the octane rating close to 100). Second, superchargers were to be banned. Oddly enough, the countries which made these proposals appeared to have most to lose from their adoption.

The fuel proposal was made by the British delegation, yet a high octane fuel was essential if high performance output was to be extracted from single-cylinder engines. The supercharger ban was urged by the Italians, despite the fact that their best hope for a title seemed to lie in the blown, water-cooled Gileras which had survived the war.

The ban certainly killed off the Gileras and it was thought to have effectively wiped out the two-stroke power unit as far as racing went – although, as we will see, this type of engine staged an amazing recovery in the 1960s. Suffice to say that the pre-war DKWs relied on supercharging systems and without these they were not competitive with four-stroke machines.

On the other hand, while the fuel restriction hit Norton and Velocette heavily it did not put their pre-war racers out of action completely. They were adapted for the 72 octane fuel and although they lost their edge they still won races.

In January 1947 Norton announced their team. It was to be led by Daniell, who was supported by two Irishmen, Artie Bell and Ernie Lyons. The bikes were the 1938 models and the only change made was to lower the compression ratio to cope with the new fuel. In 1938 the five-hundred ran at 10.5:1 and this compression ratio had to be dropped right down to 7.2:1 before the engines would run without overheating on their new low octane diet.

This knocked the peak power down from close to 50bhp at 6,800rpm to just over 40bhp. The three-fifty suffered equally, as did the Velocette racers. And the supercharger ban killed off the interesting 500cc twin which Velocette had completed in 1939.

This had been ridden during practising for the 1939 TT by Stanley Woods but it suffered from plug oiling and was not raced. It was an unusual design with contrarotating crankshafts which were geared together to give perfect balance. But it was heavy and without a supercharger it was unlikely to be able to challenge for top honours. In any case Velocette had their successful singles and the 'Roarer', as the twin was known, was not developed.

Above: probably the greatest name of the years between the wars was Stanley Woods, seen here flat out on a 350cc Velocette during the 1939 Junior TT. Although he survived the war he did not return to racing.
Right: Les Graham, first man to win the 500cc world championship, sets out for a lap of honour on his AJS after winning the class at the Swiss Grand Prix.

Above: first completely new engine to make its mark in post-war racing was the 500cc AJS, nicknamed the 'Porcupine' because of the spikey cylinder-head finning.
Right: after the war the classic round of road races was revived in 1947, when one of the first events to be held was the Belgian GP on the traditional Spa-Francorchamps circuit in the Ardennes. Here Fergus Anderson (Velocette) leads eventual winner Ken Bills (Norton) onto the Eau Rouge bridge at the start of the 350cc race.

The supercharger ban also posed problems for another new British racer. This had been designed towards the end of the war and work had started on it in 1945. At first this was to have been called a Sunbeam but when Associated Motor Cycles sold the name to the BSA group the racer was retained and was re-named an AJS.

This was the bike that became world famous as the 'Porcupine' and which carried Les Graham to World Championship honours in 1949. It caused a sensation when it was wheeled out at the first post war TT in 1947, for it was the only completely new factory racing machine in the 500cc class.

A few international events had been run in 1946 but it was not until 1947 that the sport really started to get back to normal. That year six recognised classics were run, although there was no championship of any sort. The pre-war system had been completely forgotten and each major race was run as a separate event.

Incredibly enough the year started with a clash. Although there were so few classics the organisers of the Swiss Grand Prix, which was also the Grand Prix d'Europe that year, and the Isle of Man TT both insisted on holding their races in early June. The dates were so close that it was virtually impossible for a competitor to

race in both and the interests of the factories were split down the middle with the Italians going to Switzerland and the British supporting the TT.

The 500cc Senior TT was a three cornered fight between the pre-war Norton and Velocette singles and the glittering new AJS twins. These were powered by double overhead camshaft engines with the cylinders jutting forward (the spikey finning on the cylinder heads gave the machines the name 'Porcupine').

The four-speed gearbox was in unit and the neat power plant was mounted in a brand new duplex frame, with wide splayed tubes running under the engine. Weight was a creditable 320lb without fuel and oil. It appeared a very modern machine alongside the pre-war singles.

But the singles scored on reliability and Daniell on a Norton won the race from team-mate Bell with Peter Goodman on a Velocette third.

MICHAEL TURNER

Old and the new at the 1949 Senior TT. On the left Harold Daniell with the basically pre-war factory Norton prepares to start alongside Les Graham with the far more modern AJS 'Porcupine'.

Daniell's average speed of 82.81 mph was almost exactly 7 mph down on the record for the race set in 1939 by Georg Meier of Germany on a supercharged works BMW and the fastest lap, put up jointly by Bell and Goodman at 84.07 mph, compared with the absolute lap record of 91.00 mph set by Daniell on his factory Norton in 1938. Pool petrol was certainly proving a handicap!

The poor fuel hampered the Velocettes less than the Nortons in the 350cc Junior TT, which Les Archer won. In the 250cc race Irishman Manliff Barrington on a Moto Guzzi got the verdict over Maurice Cann, though many thought that the time-keepers had got it all wrong and that Cann had in fact won.

In Switzerland Moto Guzzi dominated the 500cc class with that spectacular star of pre-war days, Omobono Tenni, winning on one of the mighty vee-twins, the machine developed from the model on which Stanley Woods won the 1935 Senior TT. Fergus Anderson kept the British flag flying in the 350cc event which he won on a Velocette but Moto Guzzi brought their total of victories to three with Bruno Francisco winning the 250cc race and Luigi Cavanna, who later became a monk, the sidecar class.

The British and Italian factories clashed for the first time since 1939 at the Dutch TT, held on the long and very fast circuit near Assen that was to be replaced in 1955 by the short course used today. The new unsupercharged air-cooled Gileras were not ready and the British factories had a good day. Bell won the 500cc class at 84.53 mph from Oscar Clemencich on a single cylinder Gilera and Goodman again scored in the 350cc class, beating Ken Bills, who had replaced Lyons in the Norton squad, by just four seconds.

The Belgian Grand Prix, run on the famous circuit at Spa-Francorchamps, saw an overwhelming Norton triumph. Bikes from the British factory won all three races held that day, with Daniell back in control in the big race, Bills winning the 350cc and Belgian champion Frans Vanderschrick top man in the sidecar class, always a favourite race at the Belgian meeting.

Fastest of the classics was the Ulster. Bell won the 500cc class at an average of 91.25 mph, with a fastest lap of 94.79 mph on the old Clady circuit, which included a bumpy seven-mile straight. Best through the speed trap was Foster on a Velocette, at 111 mph, which suggests that the

Above: top Norton rider of the late 1940s was Ulster's Artie Bell seen here in action during the 1947 Senior TT in which he finished second.

Left: Italian star Omobono Tenni in action during the 1947 Swiss Grand Prix on a 250cc factory Moto Guzzi.

Opposite: first clash between British and Italian factory teams after the war came at the 1947 Dutch TT. Here Harold Daniell (Norton) leads the 500cc class on the brick surfaced course.

true flat out speeds of the top five hundreds in 1947 was about 120mph under the best possible conditions – downhill and with a following wind!

The 500cc race lasted nearly three hours and with the races run concurrently in the style favoured before the war, Norton recruited Johnny Lockett to team with Bell in the 350cc class. He responded by winning it. In the 250cc class Cann proved that those who had doubted the TT time-keepers were probably right by beating Barrington, both riding Moto Guzzis.

Norton went to Monza for the final classic of the year, the Italian Grand Prix but they did not have much luck. Bell retired with engine trouble, Daniell crashed but remounted to finish third in the 500cc race, which was won by Arciso Artesiani on a Gilera.

The year had been no more than a limbering up exercise, with the British factories taking advantage of the ban on blowers to gain the major share of the honours while the Italians concentrated on developing new models. Overall, the economic situation cast a damper on the sport as manufacturers struggled to get production of roadsters flowing despite shortages of materials, machine tools and skilled labour.

At the end of the year things were so grim that the fuel ration in Britain was cut to nothing – you could not even ride your motor-cycle on the roads unless you were in an occupation regarded as essential and thus qualified for a fuel ration. It is difficult to envisage in these relatively bountiful years just how tough things were in Europe in those immediate post war years.

THE CLASSIC ROUND

Things brightened a little in 1948. In Britain a petrol ration of 9 gallons for six months for machines under 250cc and 13 for 250cc and larger bikes was introduced (half a gallon a week!) and the first brand new racer which could be bought by private owners was announced. This was the 350cc 7R AJS, which was to continue in production right up until 1962 and with the Manx Norton was to be one of the mainstays of the class.

In 1948 it was an advanced machine. The 348cc engine (bore and stroke 74 × 81mm) had a chain driven overhead camshaft, light alloy head and barrel and a magnesium alloy crankcase.

Running on the 72 octane fuel with a compression ratio of 8.5:1 it revved to 7,000. The frame was advanced too, with swinging fork rear suspension and telescopic front fork (a racing version of hydraulically damped Teledraulic which had become famous on the war-time 350cc AJS/Matchless models). The 7R had a top speed of just over 100mph.

There was still no sign of a championship series and the classic round consisted of the same six events. That year the Swiss race was moved forward in the calendar to early May to avoid a clash with the TT and was run on a short course at Geneva, not at Berne. The new Gileras were still not ready and Daniell and Bell had little trouble in beating the best that Moto Guzzi could field to score another 1–2 for Norton.

Bell won the 350cc race and with Dario Ambrosini winning the 250cc class on a works Benelli it was a black day for Moto Guzzi. In fact their record of three wins, set the previous year, was equalled by Norton, with Hans Haldemann of Switzerland winning the sidecar race.

It was very nearly a different story at the TT. Omobono Tenni, riding a vee-twin Moto Guzzi, set such a pace in the Senior TT that no one could stay with him. After the first lap the little Italian led by 29 seconds and from a standing start he had pushed the 'pool' fuel lap record from 84.07 to 87.60mph. Despite a pit stop to change a plug Tenni held the lead until he encountered more plug trouble and then ran out of fuel on lap five. Bell won the race at 84.97 mph, with Tenni making fastest lap at 88.06mph.

It was not a good TT for Norton. They were lucky to win the Senior after being outpaced by Tenni and in the 350cc race their riders could not catch the best of the Velocettes. That race was won by Freddie Frith, who ironically had made his name before the war on Nortons, with Bob Foster on another Velocette in second place.

The new 7R AJS showed up well, with Maurice Cann finishing fifth though the works entered bikes fell by the wayside. Cann, back on his home-tuned Moto Guzzi, won the 250cc race which was noteworthy because for the first time in the Isle of Man a mass start was employed. But with only 25 starters on relatively slow bikes little was proved by this experiment.

Riding in the Isle of Man for the first time that year was a youngster named Geoff Duke. He led a race on a works Norton until he got stuck in a mud-hole! The event was the Isle of Man Grand National Scramble, held that year near Windy Corner, and Duke's mount was a push-rod 500T

The British AJS factory did racing a great service when they produced the 350cc 7R model for sale in 1948. This fast and reliable machine soon became one of the mainstays of the class and remained in production until 1962.

Above: Hans Haldemann hurls his Norton into a corner during the 1949 Swiss Grand Prix with his passenger, by today's standards, in a rather unusual position. Haldemann was one of the great aces of sidecar racing.

Below: surprise packet of the 1948 Senior TT was Omobono Tenni on a works vee-twin Moto Guzzi. Despite plug troubles he led the race until he ran out of fuel. Here the little Italian leaps the big Moto Guzzi over Ballaugh Bridge.

Norton scrambler. Two years later he returned
to dominate the TT.

The new four-cylinder Gileras were ready for
the Dutch TT, where two were out in practice.
Only Masserini rode one in the 500cc race, however, when he shot ahead from the start and led
Bell at the end of the first lap. With a fastest lap
at 87.75mph Bell passed the Gilera and went on
to win. Masserini slid off when rain fell, leaving
Nello Pagani to finish second on a single-cylinder
Gilera ahead of Jock West on an AJS 'Porcupine'

The new Gilera was very light (it was claimed
to weigh under 300lbs). The neat unit construc-
tion air-cooled engine with cylinders in line was
set across the frame and drive was via a four-
speed gearbox in unit with the engine. Power was
about 50bhp at 8,500rpm but the handling did
not match the engine. The front fork was of pre-

war pressed steel blade type while the rear
swinging fork was controlled by an unusual
system of bell cranks and springs which was soon
scrapped.

The British and Italian factories did not clash
at the Belgian that year. The Italians preferred
to compete in a meeting at Berne in Switzerland
and it was there that Tenni, so recently the hero of
the TT, was killed when he crashed during practice.

This led to an all-British battle in Belgium and
this time the AJS team very nearly pulled it off.
The 'Porcupine' was clearly faster than the
Norton but Les Graham's luck was out as usual,
and he retired with a misfire after lapping at
93.75mph. Johnny Lockett, third man in the
Norton team, was the victor from Jock West
(AJS). In the 350cc race winner Bob Foster
(Velocette) made history by beating the pre-war

Above: dramatic moment from the storm lashed 1948 Ulster Grand Prix as Artie Bell (Norton) hits the bank. Enrico Lorenzetti (Moto Guzzi, *left*) went on to win.
Left: the air-cooled four-cylinder 500cc Gilera first appeared in 1948. Carlo Bandirola is the rider.

lap record. This was the first time that this had been achieved on a classic circuit during the era of low octane fuel; Foster's speed of 90.37mph compared with 89.48mph set by Stanley Woods (Velocette) in 1939.

Although the Ulster race was the Grand Prix of Europe that year few of the Italians made the trip – and when they learned that the race was held in pouring rain they were probably pleased they had not bothered. The Ulster was still run in the old style, over a long distance with all three classes on the circuit at the same time.

The big race developed into a grim, sodden battle between Bell on the leading works Norton and Enrico Lorenzetti on a factory single-cylinder Moto Guzzi. Eventually the frame of Bell's Norton broke and Lorenzetti kept going to win.

The Italian Grand Prix, scheduled as a classic,

was something of a damp squib. It was switched from its traditional home at Monza to a short circuit at Faenza; no 350cc race was run and it clashed with the International Six Days Trial and the Manx Grand Prix. These factors resulted in a lack of British interest and the event was supported only by the Italian factories.

The result of the 500cc race was nevertheless significant, for it was won by Masserini on a four-cylinder Gilera, who beat Ulster winner Lorenzetti on the works single-cylinder Moto Guzzi. The Gilera challenge was taking shape.

Right at the end of the year the FICM decided to re-introduce a championship system. This was agreed at the Autumn Congress held in London in November. But instead of calling the titles 'European' it was decided to go the whole hog and dub them 'World' championships.

The scoring system included a point for the fastest lap (dropped after 1949) and the usual six classics counted for the 1949 championships. The stage was set and the time to restart a title series was appropriate, for with two seasons of racing behind them the factories were well prepared for the fray.

NEW DESIGNS TRIUMPH

The introduction of the world championships coincided with a complete change of fortunes in the all-important 500cc class. Previously the old Nortons, modified pre-war bikes, had virtually ruled the roost. But in 1949 the new breed of multis took over and the AJS 'Porcupine', which until then had promised so much but achieved little, really came into its own.

AJS had a strong team led by former RAF pilot Les Graham, supported by determined Bill Doran and reliable Ted Frend. During two seasons of racing most of the bugs had been sorted out of the machines and although they were not as fast as the Gileras, superior riding and reliability won them the first ever 500cc world championship.

Graham won the class at the Swiss, finished second to Pagani (Gilera) in the Dutch, retired with a split tank in the Belgian, led the Senior TT until magneto trouble just two miles from the finish, and clinched the title by winning the Ulster. Then to underline his success Graham went to Monza and was fighting for the lead with Carlo Bandirola (Gilera) when the Italian crashed. The Gilera bounced into the AJS and Graham came down too. Bandirola's team-mates Pagani and Artesiani went on to finish first and second.

Doran had won the Belgian, nipping ahead of Artesiani and Lorenzetti (Moto Guzzi) on the last corner, so the year ended with the score: AJS 3 wins, Gilera 2, and Norton 1. The Norton success had been scored by Harold Daniell, the South Londoner who had started racing in the Isle of Man in 1930!

He won the Senior TT simply because he kept going while the faster multis faded out. Clearly the old Nortons were finished and if the team wanted to keep in the hunt new racers would have to be produced. There were rumours of four-cylinder designs but the machines that eventually appeared at the start of the 1950 season were completely new single-cylinder racers, the model which became famous the world over as the 'Featherbed'.

In a single jump Norton had moved from a

Historic moment as the two men chiefly concerned with the creation of the factory featherbed Nortons pose with the original 500cc model in 1950. Norton's race chief Joe Craig is on the left, Rex McCandless is on the right.

design that was very distinctly pre-war to one which, with fairly minor modifications, would still be giving a good account of itself through the 1960s. The new 'Featherbed' was the brain child of Rex McCandless of Belfast, and its introduction coincided with two other milestones: first, an increase of the octane rating of permitted fuel to 80, secondly the arrival of Geoff Duke on the international scene.

Top: within weeks of Geoff Duke joining the official Norton team, the 'featherbed' made its debut in a minor meeting at Blandford in Dorset in April 1950. Here Duke gets down to it in characteristic style while winning the 500cc race.

Below: Artie Bell's career ended when he was involved in a multiple pile-up during the 500cc race at the Belgian Grand Prix in 1950. His Norton (nearest camera) and Les Graham's AJS finished up like this. No one was killed.

Duke had started his career as a trials rider and scrambler. He joined the Norton trials team in 1948 and first raced on the TT course in the 350cc Manx Grand Prix (the race for non-international riders) the same year, taking the lead on the fourth lap before a broken oil pipe put him out.

He returned in 1949 to finish second in the 350cc race and to win the 500cc event. With Daniell ready to retire Duke was signed by Norton for the 1950 season, teaming with Bell, Lockett and Daniell, who competed in the TT before retiring.

From the word go Duke was a sensation. Clad in the trim fitting one-piece leathers which are now universal wear he looked as if he belonged to a different generation from his rivals, who wore rather baggy two-piece suits. As he took every advantage of the superb road holding of the 'Featherbed' his style was breath-taking – Duke swept into corners faster than any rider ever had

before, and he laid the Norton over to angles that had crowds gasping.

But for tyre trouble this first-year international from Lancashire would certainly have won the 500cc world championship. He waltzed away with the TT, shattering the pre-war average speed and lap record, which he upped from Daniell's 91.00mph to a searing 93.33mph, but in Belgium the tread stripped off his rear tyre when he had the Gilera team well beaten.

Bell's career had ended at the same meeting. He was involved in a crash and received injuries which put him out of the sport.

Another milestone was recorded at that Belgian meeting, where MV Agusta contested the 500cc class of a classic for the first time. Their machine was a Gilera-style four with torsion bar rear springing and shaft drive.

Dunlop flew out new tyres for the Dutch TT, the weekend after the Belgian, but someone had got their sums wrong and these proved to be worse than the original covers. Within a few laps the complete AJS and Norton teams were out, Duke crashing heavily when the tread stripped and locked the rear wheel just as he was braking heavily. Umberto Masetti, a newcomer to the Gilera team, won the 500cc class in both Belgium and Holland.

Graham (AJS) won the big class at the Swiss Grand Prix, where the Norton team (back to

Left: Carlo Bandirola in action on the original MV Agusta 500cc racer. In 1950 MV Agusta contested the big class for the first time. Their machine was very similar to the Gilera and the four-cylinder double-overhead camshaft engine had in fact been designed by the same man, Pietro Remor. An innovation was shaft-drive but it was not successful and was later dropped in favour of a chain.
Below: airborne action from the 1950 Ulster Grand Prix as Les Graham (AJS) leads Johnny Lockett (Norton) in the 500cc race.

strength with the addition of Dickie Dale in place of Bell) was subdued after their run of troubles. For Ulster they switched to Avon tyres, a partnership that was to last until Norton quit the championship scene. In confident mood again Duke won the race and then went to Italy where he staggered the Italians by easily beating the Gilera and MV Agusta teams.

This victory clinched the manufacturers' world championship for Norton but in the riders' championship it was not enough to make up for those disasters in Belgium and Holland – Gilera's Masetti took the individual title from Duke by a single point. . . .

The single-cylinder engine, so often condemned as out of date, was back in business in a big way. Joe Craig, technical master-mind at the Norton factory, had worked this miracle, assisted by the new McCandless frame and the phenomenon known as Duke.

Such a combination of talent could not be denied. In 1951 Duke failed to score in the first two classics (missing the newly promoted Spanish which opened the series and retiring from the Swiss with ignition failure) but then shattered the opposition to win the TT, Belgian and Dutch races in quick succession. A win at the Ulster clinched the title, but at Monza Duke and his

Above: single cylinder against the multis at the 1951 Dutch TT – and the single won. Here Fergus Anderson leads on a twin-cylinder Moto Guzzi from Umberto Masetti (Gilera) but Geoff Duke (Norton, *right*) came through to win.
Left: Eric Oliver was undisputed top man in the sidecar class in the early years of the world championships. Here with Italian passenger Lorenzo Dobelli he corners their Norton during the 1952 Spanish Grand Prix.
Below, left: Dario Ambrosini kept the Benelli flag flying in the 250cc class until his death in 1951.

Norton were trounced by the Gilera riders who took the first three places.

Duke also won the 350cc title, at last breaking the grip of Velocette whose machines had dominated the class since the resumption of racing after the war. And for the third year running Eric Oliver had taken the sidecar title so that in 1951 Norton had the distinction of winning three titles.

The 250cc championship had, during the first two years of the championships, been a straight fight between Moto Guzzi and Dario Ambrosini on the lone works Benelli. In 1950 Ambrosini had triumphed but a fatal crash while practising for the French Grand Prix at Albi in 1951 left the field clear for Moto Guzzi, who made technical history that year by fitting their works machines with five-speed gearboxes – the first step in the race for more ratios.

GOLDEN AGE

The Gilera clean sweep at Monza at the end of the 1951 season was clear writing on the wall. Joe Craig had wrung more power from the single – and he was to get even more – but the Italians were not only fighting and winning the technical battle. Their approach to riders was entirely different from that taken by the British manufacturers, particularly Norton.

Realising that it was ridiculous to spend thousands of pounds developing new machines and then to offer star riders only a normal wage to race them the Italians were willing to pay big money to attract the men who had beaten them, the top British riders.

Even more important they treated the riders as equals – not as hired jockeys. The first world champion to make the switch was Les Graham: after winning the 500cc title for AJS in 1949 he raced for one more season with the British company, and then joined MV Agusta for 1951.

Next target for the Italians was obviously Geoff Duke. He was clearly the best rider in the world and to have him in a team would give it an advantage that rivals could compensate for only with several extra brake horse power. If a team had indisputably the best machine in the world, as the Gilera was, and Duke could be persuaded to ride it, then the combination would be very very difficult to beat.

With talk of big money being earned by the riders under contract to Italian factories it was natural that Duke should become restless. Yet he was patriotic and he decided to ride for Norton again in 1952. He easily won the 350cc title again, scoring four wins in a row, but in the 500cc class the going was tough.

The Gilera was miles an hour faster and Masetti could sit with him and then, with a twist of the throttle, clear off to win – which he did in both the Dutch TT and the Belgian GP. The TT was a bitter disappointment for Duke. Despite mis-firing at high revs he was well in the lead when the clutch failed, forcing him to retire.

Because he loved racing Duke insisted on riding in non-championship events. The West Germans had been re-admitted to the FIM (the name of the governing body had been changed in 1949 from the Fédération Internationale des Clubs Motocycliste to the more straightforward Fédération Internationale Motocycliste) and the organisers of a meeting at Schotten offered Duke big money to compete.

It was a dangerous course, narrow and bordered by trees. Hampered by lack of practice, Duke mistook one corner for another, crashed at speed and was very lucky to escape with only a broken arm. Norton replaced him with Rhodesian Ray Amm, who joined Ken Kavanagh and Reg Armstrong.

Duke's arm took a long time to heal and the season ended without him racing again. He was still eager to win on a British machine but it soon

Les Graham was the first British world champion to switch to Italian machinery. He joined the MV Agusta team for the 1951 season and is pictured at one of his first public appearances on the factory's 500cc four-cylinder racer.

became obvious that Norton had not pushed ahead with the design and development of a four-cylinder racer that they had been talking about. Duke felt that it was useless to race singles again, and with no hope of Norton producing a multi, he reluctantly accepted an offer to join the Gilera team for 1953.

With West Germany back in the fold, competition in the 250cc class became more intense and right at the end of the 1952 season Werner Haas on a beautifully engineered NSU twin came within a foot of winning the Italian Grand Prix. Fergus Anderson, the first British rider to 'go Italian', won the race for Moto Guzzi, but only by the closest of margins. In the 125cc class MV Agusta rejoiced as Cecil Sandford won them their first title, riding one of the neat little double overhead camshaft works racers.

Sidecar racing suffered a double blow with the deaths in racing accidents of two great Continental aces, Italy's Ercole Frigerio who raced works Gileras, and Norton-riding Belgian Frans Vanderschrick. Then Eric Oliver broke a leg in a minor French meeting and balding Cyril Smith seized his chance to win the title on a Norton.

Geoff Duke's decision to join Gilera in 1953 was a shattering blow for the British enthusiasts of the day – especially as Reg Armstrong went with him to the Italian team. But Norton re-grouped and Ray Amm took over as the leader with support from Kavanagh and Jack Brett. The line up for the Senior TT that year was one of the best ever: Duke, Armstrong and Dickie Dale on Gileras, Les Graham and Bandirola on MV Agustas, Walter Zeller on a fuel-injection works BMW, the Norton team and the AJS squad led by New Zealander Rod Coleman on the re-designed 'Porcupine', now with the engine tilted up at 45 degrees and without those spiky cylinder head fins that had given it its name.

Duke started with a record lap at 96.38mph and led from Graham, Amm and Kavanagh. Then on lap two tragedy struck. Graham lost control of the unwieldy looking MV Agusta as he screamed down Bray Hill at 130mph. He lost his life in the ensuing crash and the sparkle went out of the race. Amm took up the challenge. Duke responded with another lap record at 97.20mph and Amm promptly topped this with a round at 97.41mph!

Top: by 1952 the improved Gilera was more than a match for the Norton in the 500cc class, as Geoff Duke (Norton) finds as he tries to catch Umberto Masetti (Gilera) during the Dutch TT that year.
Centre: another moment from the Gilera–Norton battles of that year as Duke leads from Ray Amm (Norton), Masetti and Alfredo Milani (Gilera) at the Belgian Grand Prix. Again Masetti was the winner.
Bottom: when Duke was injured in 1952 Rhodesian Ray Amm became a full-time member of the Norton team.

Dale and Zeller slid off on wet tar at Signpost – and Duke dropped it at Quarter Bridge. He opened the throttle just a shade too quickly and the sudden surge of power flipped the Gilera sideways. The tank was too damaged for him to continue and Amm went on his way to win, completing the double that he had started earlier in the week by winning the 350cc race.

Amm crashed heavily when leading the 350cc French Grand Prix, breaking a collar-bone.

Above: Geoff Duke had his first ride on a 500cc four-cylinder Gilera when he tested one of the factory machines at Monza in May 1953. It was the start of an association that was to dominate the big class for three seasons.
Below: impressive line-up for a race at Hockenheim in 1953. Nearest the camera is Fergus Anderson on the in-line four-cylinder Moto Guzzi. Next to him is Les Graham on the unwieldy looking MV Agusta.

That virtually ended the Norton challenge for the year for although Kavanagh won the big class at the Ulster, taking over when Duke was slowed by clutch trouble, the new Moto Guzzi singles outpaced the British singles in the 350cc division while the Gileras lived up to their early promise by winning the 500cc class of the Dutch, Belgian, French, Swiss and Italian classics.

Duke won four of these to emerge as the world champion, and with Armstrong in second place the Gilera supremacy was complete. Anderson and Lorenzetti took the first two places in the 350cc division on their 'overgrown' Moto Guzzis, but in the 250cc division the Italians took a knock.

There NSU were unbeatable and to complete a neat and tidy double in the lightweight classes little Werner Haas won both the 125cc and 250cc world championships. This was the West German factory's first real attempt at championship racing and their single-cylinder overhead-camshaft 125cc racer and 250cc twin set new standards.

This was a period of intense development. Moto Guzzi were experimenting with a 500cc water-cooled four-cylinder racer with the cylinders in line with the direction of travel – not set across the frame as in the Gilera and MV Agusta – and shaft drive. However, handling problems caused by the effect of the longitudinally placed crankshaft, which imparted a twisting motion to the whole machine, were never overcome and it was later abandoned.

Every constructor was experimenting with streamlining. The Italians had been using this,

especially on 125cc machines, at Monza for some time. And at Monza at the end of the year Walter Zeller's 500cc BMW appeared with comprehensive streamlining which completely shrouded the front and much of the rear wheel too.

Norton went the whole hog. They built a really revolutionary and very low machine that was designed from start to finish as a streamlined racer – as opposed to an orthodox bike with the streamlining tacked on afterwards. The rider

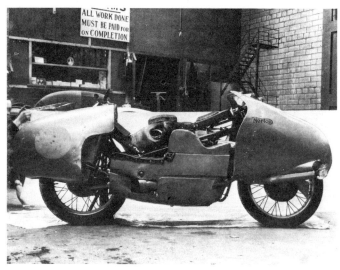

Above: Norton introduced this unorthodox machine with kneeling riding position as an experiment in 1953. To get a really low riding position fuel was carried in pannier tanks below the rider's arm. Ray Amm tried it in practice but never raced it in a world championship event.
Below: sidecar action at the Belgian Grand Prix in 1953 as Eric Oliver (Norton) leads Cyril Smith (Norton) and Willi Faust (BMW). They finished in that order.

knelt, as sidecar racers do, and the fuel was carried in pannier tanks fitting under his arms.

This 'secret weapon' was tried by Amm during practice for the TT (fitted with a 350cc engine) and again at the Dutch TT. But it was never raced in a classic because Amm established that he could not better his lap times set with the orthodox machine, as he found the streamliner more difficult to control. However at the end of 1953 Norton took the 'Flying Fish' to the Montlhéry track near Paris and, with the engines running on alcohol fuel, shattered a whole crop of world records.

Most impressive was the hour into which Amm packed just over 133 miles. He also set a motorcycle lap record for the circuit at 145mph. Clearly streamlining had a lot to offer – provided that it did not affect handling too much.

Oliver was back in control in the sidecar class, winning four of the five classics and starting a revolution when he wheeled out a comprehensively streamlined outfit during practice for the Belgian Grand Prix. This had a kneeling riding position and had been built for him by Watsonian Sidecars of Birmingham; it was powered by a Norton factory engine. It was not the first 'kneeler', but it was the first to be raced by a star and it set a new trend.

Oliver did not race the outfit in a classic until 1954, when it had been improved; Oliver won the first three classics in a row – then broke his arm competing in a minor meeting in West Germany. Despite this he made a heroic attempt to keep his title by riding in the Swiss Grand Prix before he was fit. But not even Oliver could win with a

broken arm and the steadily mounting challenge of the factory-backed BMW riders was rewarded with studious looking Wilhelm Noll winning the championship for West Germany.

Although nobody realized it at the time, 1954 was the final year of big-time Norton support for the classics – and the machine that they produced for the year was one of the classic racers of all time. Over the years the bore and stroke of the 500cc racer had changed, with the bore getting progressively larger and the stroke shorter. The original five-hundred of the mid-thirties had a bore and stroke of 79 × 100mm. In 1938 new engines were built with 82 × 94mm dimensions. These were retained until 1952 when 'square' engines with 85.9 × 86mm were introduced. The next year the bore/stroke ratio was modified again, going well over-square at 88 × 82mm.

The final version of the works 500cc Norton, built for the 1954 season, was even more over-square with a 90mm bore and a stroke of 78.4mm. To get sufficient fly-wheel effect an outside fly-wheel was fitted. The engine revved to 8,000rpm and produced, on the conversative Norton brake, 55bhp. In the intervening years it is extremely doubtful if anyone has got more power out of a single-cylinder five-hundred running on petrol than Joe Craig did that year.

At the same time Norton produced a new three-fifty with 78 × 73mm bore and stroke. They experimented with a five-speed gearbox on the five-hundred but this was a failure and was not sufficiently reliable to be used. Oil cooling of the exhaust valve was retained, a new front-brake with cast-in hot air extractor fan fitted and Amm's machine was equipped with distinctive streamlining, with a long 'nose' sticking out over the front wheel.

Amm again led the team with Brett in support and Australian Gordon Laing on the third bike. Opposing them in the 500cc class was the formidable Gilera line-up headed by Duke, Masetti and Armstrong. MV Agusta had signed Dale, Bandirola and Lomas while Moto Guzzi relied on Kavanagh, Anderson and Lorenzetti, who raced brand new super-streamlined, very light single-cylinder machines in preference to the in-line four. AJS were in the hunt with Coleman and Bob McIntyre on their bikes – a total of five works teams who, between them, sometimes fielded up to 20 factory bikes in a single race, no wonder this became known as a Golden Age!

Left: at the end of the successful 1953 season Geoff Duke signed a contract for a further year with the Gilera factory – Giuseppe Gilera, boss of the famous Italian works, is on the right, team-manager Piero Taruffi left.
Below: in 1954 Bob McIntyre joined the AJS team. That year the London-built racers achieved a new low profile by using pannier tanks with a fuel pump to lift petrol to the carburetters. McIntyre is on the 350cc model.

END OF AN ERA

In 1954 an era was drawing to a close. Amm and Norton started well with wins in the 500cc TT and Ulster Grand Prix, held that year immediately after the Isle of Man race. However, the TT was cut short because of rain, and when the riders were suddenly flagged off after only four laps, Duke was lying a handy second and many thought that he could have won the race.

Gilera did not go to Ulster, but after that race Duke won the 500cc class of the Belgian, Dutch, German, Swiss and Italian Grands Prix in succession, to gain the world championship for the third time. Amm finished second, the combination of the Rhodesian and the Norton proving more than a match for all but Duke and his Gilera.

Amm also finished second in the 350cc championship, beaten only by Anderson (Moto Guzzi). NSU were virtually unopposed in the 250cc class, Haas leading the team to a 1–2–3 in grand prix after grand prix, while in the 125cc class his team-mate Rupert Hollaus from Austria won the title.

During the year the streamlining on the NSUs had grown from a neat dolphin fairing that left the front wheel exposed to a full 'dustbin' of the type pioneered by Moto Guzzi. Even Gilera adopted full streamlining at the end of the year. Duke appeared at Monza with his Gilera partly hidden by a light alloy streamlining that enclosed the front wheel and extended back to his legs.

Neither riders nor spectators were happy about these large and cumbersome fairings. The riders objected because handling, particularly in windy conditions, was affected. Spectators did not like them because they hid so much of the machines from view. But they were worth several brake horsepower and increased top-end speed by up to 10mph, so that factory teams had no alternative but to use them.

Racing machines were getting too expensive and too far removed from roadsters, at least in the opinion of a number of manufacturers. The British makers particularly objected to the new trend towards streamlining, and they were also conscious of the fact that they would have to

A familiar sight in 1954: Ray Amm on the 500cc works Norton with streamlined 'nose'. The Rhodesian won the Senior TT and despite the 'multis' he finished second to Duke in the world championship series.

spend a tremendous amount of money to build completely new racers if they wanted to stay in the hunt.

Apart from publicity these would have no commercial value. The lessons learned from developing a four- or six-cylinder racer can seldom be included in a catalogue sports model on sale to the public. Coupled with this, the demand for motorcycles, particularly in the European market, was levelling off, and the two factors prompted Norton, AJS and NSU to withdraw from racing.

At one stroke racing had lost three of the factories which had given tremendous support. Both Norton and AJS continued to compete on a greatly reduced scale with teams of riders on specially prepared versions of their catalogued racing machines, the 350 and 500cc Manx Norton and the 350cc AJS and 500cc G45 Matchless, but the great days of British factory teams were over.

NSU took a similar line. They sold a single-cylinder 250cc racer, named the Sportmax, which soon became a 'must' for the serious privateer contesting the class. Their fabulous works

During the 1953 and 1954 seasons rapid progress was made with streamlining, well illustrated by these three shots of Werner Haas of the German NSU team. At the top Haas is seen winning the 1953 250cc TT, his NSU carrying only a small nose fairing. Early in the following year Haas is pictured in action at the French Grand Prix (*centre*) with far more comprehensive streamlining on the machine.
Above: final step was to enclose the front wheel. This was done for the Dutch TT in June.

machines became museum pieces while they were still capable of beating anything in the 125cc and 250cc classes.

The final 125cc NSU was powered by a single cylinder double overhead camshaft engine with very much over-square bore and stroke (58 × 47.3), which revved to 11,500rpm and produced about 20bhp. The even more impressive two-fifty, on which Haas averaged 90.88mph while winning the 250cc TT (a speed which would have placed him second in the 350cc race that year!) had 55.9 × 50.8mm dimensions and produced 39bhp, also at 11,500rpm. NSU also led the trend to gearboxes with more ratios, fitting both machines with six-speed boxes.

In fact 1954 was a year when gearboxes were in the news. Gilera and MV both fitted five-speeders to their 500cc four-cylinder racers, Moto Guzzi had five-speeders on all their racing machines and, like NSU, MV went to a six-speeder on their 125cc machine.

With Norton out of racing, Ray Amm joined MV but was killed in his first race for the Italian factory, at Imola when he was chasing Kavanagh (Guzzi) on the new 350cc four-cylinder MV. This was a dismal start to the 1955 season.

It was not in fact a happy season. Poor starting money at the Dutch TT led to the famous 'riders' strike'. The basic wage of the Continental Circus rider is the agreed fee he gets for starting in the races; it is usually a very low figure and is hardly enough to cover day-to-day living costs. Requests for more starting money were turned down, and the riders agreed to pull in after completing a single lap of the 350cc race. Together with several works riders who supported them, including Duke and Armstrong, they were later disciplined by the FIM. They were 'tried' by an FIM court and were suspended for the first six months of the 1956 season.

It was a scandalous business and reflected no credit at all on the FIM. But as the majority of people connected with this body were, and still are, organisers of race meetings it was entirely predictable. The FIM was terrified by the prospect of the riders getting together and organising themselves so as to obtain a fair scale of starting money. They still are!

But apart from the 350cc class of the Dutch TT, this had no bearing on the 1955 season. Gilera quite often ran six of their 500cc fours in a race, and Duke rode them to win four classics in a row and took the championship for the fourth time. At the end of the year, however, Gilera got a shock when Masetti, who had switched camps, just beat them at Monza in the Italian Grand Prix. It had taken a long time but at long last the big MV was showing promise.

Originally Bill Lomas was to have raced the 'new policy' AJS and Matchless racers. However after a disagreement at the TT Lomas switched

Above: start of the 350cc class at the Belgian Grand Prix in 1957. By this time fully streamlined machines were used by all the leading riders. Winner of the race was Australian Keith Campbell (Moto Guzzi) nearest camera. Next to him is Libero Liberati (Gilera), then Bob Brown (Gilera), Alano Montanari (Moto Guzzi), John Surtees (MV Agusta) and Arthur Wheeler (Moto Guzzi).
Left: Tarquinio Provini and his Mondial after his win in the 125cc TT in 1957. With him is Carlo Ubbiali (MV).

to the Guzzi team for the 350cc class while riding for MV in the 250cc, a rather unique arrangement as two factories were deadly rivals. He ended the year the 350cc champion and very nearly took the 250cc title as well.

Lomas finished first in the 250cc class of the Dutch TT but because he had not stopped his engine when he refuelled he was excluded from the results – and the points that he lost meant that the title went to West German Hermann Muller, the 45 year old veteran who started racing in 1931 and who drove the famous rear-engined Auto Union Grand Prix cars in the late 1930s. Muller rode one of the new single-cylinder NSU Sportmax models, with factory backing.

Top, left: whew! Dickie Dale breathes a sigh of relief after finishing the 1957 Senior TT on a vee-eight Moto Guzzi. Despite troubles Dale finished fourth.
Above: Ray Amm prepares for his first race on a works MV Agusta at Imola in 1955. During the race he crashed and died from the injuries he received.
Left: one of the unusual engines of the 1950s was the three-cylinder two-stroke DKW. The two outer cylinders were vertical with the middle cylinder projecting forward.

Chief rival to Moto Guzzi in the 350cc class were the unusual three-cylinder two-stroke DKW works machines. These had first appeared in 1952 but did not become really competitive until 1955. The air-cooled engine of this DKW was set across the frame, with the centre cylinder jutting straight forward with the outboard ones nearly vertical. Bore and stroke were almost 'square' at 53×52.8mm. By 1955 the engines were giving 42bhp and this output, coupled with an incredibly low weight (about 200lb) and low build made them a threat, especially on twisty circuits. August Hobl rode one to finish third in the championship.

Technical sensation of the year was the eight-cylinder 500cc Guzzi, a machine still spoken about in hushed tones. In fact it was never a great success, although as an engineering exercise it is still outstanding. The water-cooled vee-eight engine was set across the frame with gear primary drive to the unit-construction gearbox which could be fitted with four, five or six speed internals to suit circuit and rider choice.

The eight Dell'Orto carburetters criss-crossed in the centre of the block, between the two banks of cylinders, each of which had an individual exhaust pipe. Bore and stroke of the very compact unit were 44×41mm and power output of the original unit was about 65bhp at 12,000rpm. Later this was increased to almost 80bhp.

The vee-eight first appeared at the Belgian Grand Prix, where it was only tried in practice and it did not begin to make its mark until 1956. That season started under a pall, for Duke, Armstrong and a dozen top line private riders were under suspension.

One bright spot was that John Surtees, after a brilliant season on the 'over the counter' works Norton racers, had joined the MV team to race the 350cc and 500cc four-cylinder machines. The bigger machine was already competitive and, aided by advice from Surtees, it was an even better bike by the time the 1956 classic season got under way.

The Earles forks had been dropped in favour of straightforward telescopic forks. The 500cc four-cylinder engine (52 × 58mm) pushed out about 65bhp at 10,500rpm to give a top speed of about 150mph on the faster circuits. The 350cc version (47.5 × 49mm) gave 48bhp at 11,000rpm, but at 345lb it was only 15lb lighter than its big brother and was not really a match for the single-cylinder Guzzi. This was far smaller, weighed only 265lb, and was superbly streamlined.

This superiority of the Guzzi led to Surtees' downfall. He crashed heavily while chasing Bill Lomas in the German Grand Prix at Solitude and broke an arm. Fortunately for him he had already won the first three 500cc Grands Prix of the year and this was enough to gain him the title.

Surtees and Duke clashed only once that year. Because of his suspension Duke's first race was the Belgian in early July. There he was leading Surtees when one of the pistons of his Gilera broke near the end of the race. Surtees won and that was that. Duke crashed on wet roads when leading the Ulster and he had to wait until the sixth and final classic to score his first championship points of 1956, in the Italian Grand Prix at Monza, where he beat team mate Libero Liberati after a great race.

The Guzzi vee-eight showed flashes of its expected form, particularly at the German where Lomas set a lap record at 95.38mph, but never kept it up long enough to win a major race. In the 350cc class the story was different: Lomas was champion again and the single-cylinder Guzzi beat off the challenge of the MV four – although at the end of the year Gilera wheeled out a 350cc version of their 'quattro' and Liberati blew everyone off to win at Monza.

Top: most complex engine ever built for motor-cycle racing was the 500cc vee-eight Moto Guzzi. This was raced from 1955 to the end of 1957. Final version gave 80bhp.
Centre: more successful than the Moto Guzzi was the four cylinder MV Agusta. Under the guidance of John Surtees this was the championship winner in 1956. This shot of Surtees starting in the Senior TT shows the bike well.
Left: flying egg! Carlo Ubbiali in action on the well streamlined 125cc MV Agusta during the 1956 Belgian GP.

Little Carlo Ubbiali was in a class of his own on the factory MVs in the lightweight categories, easily winning both titles to bring the Italian factory's score to three championships that year.

It was the twilight of the Gods. At the end of the 1957 season Gilera, Guzzi and Mondial, who had flashed onto the scene to snatch both lightweight titles from MV, pulled out of racing – without a word of warning to their riders, who first read the news in a British motor-cycle journal!

The season had started promisingly. The brilliant Scot Bob McIntyre replaced Armstrong in the Gilera team, where he teamed with Duke, Liberati and Alfredo Milani. Surtees and Masetti led the MV squad and Australian Keith Campbell had joined Lomas and Dale on the Guzzis. But DKW had faded away and although BMW again supported the talented Walter Zeller in the 500cc class they too were losing interest.

Then Duke crashed in the warming up race at Imola and a shoulder injury kept him out of action for four of the six classics. Lomas also came off at Imola and another crash, in Holland, put him out of racing for good. This seemed to

Dramatic moment in the 1957 Golden Jubilee Senior TT as Bob McIntyre (Gilera) rounds Governor's Bridge ahead of John Surtees (MV Agusta). McIntyre went on to win the race, lengthened that year to eight laps, and during it set the first-ever 100mph TT lap.

leave the coast clear for McIntyre, but a series of misfortunes plagued the Scot.

However, he did have one brilliantly successful meeting, the Golden Jubilee TT. In the Isle of Man he first won the 350cc race and then, on a never to be forgotten sunny but windy day, he shattered the 100mph lap barrier to win the 500cc Senior TT, lengthened that year from seven to eight laps. Mac's best lap was 101.12mph and his average for the 301 mile race was 98.99mph.

In the Championship, this put the McIntyre ahead of Liberati who had beaten him in the West German Grand Prix at Hockenheim despite a lap record at 129.55mph by the Scot – the fastest lap in a classic until Giacomo Agostini clocked a lap at over 130mph in the Belgian many years later. But a crash in the Dutch TT when trying to make up time lost when he stopped to cure a misfire put McIntyre out of the championship struggle.

That race was won by Surtees, but the big MV would not run properly with a full bin fairing and a week later at the ultra-fast Belgian GP circuit, where full streamlining was essential, the MV overheated and eventually blew up.

In fact the MV was really no match for the Gilera in a straight fight – but Surtees could have won the Belgian race. For without Duke or McIntyre, Gilera were relying on Liberati – and his engine failed during the warming up period. Gilera decided that Liberati should switch to the

Above: a happy moment for Geoff Duke as he is congratulated after winning the 500 cc class of the Swedish Grand Prix at Hedemora in 1958. Earlier he had won the 350 cc race. In both he rode Nortons. These proved to be Duke's last world championship wins.

Left: typical world championship scene of the 1950s as the sidecar race at the 1958 West German Grand Prix at the famous Nürburgring gets away. On the far side of the front row is the famous Swiss rider Florian Camathias (BMW) and next to him is West German Walter Schneider (BMW), twice winner of the sidecar world championship.

Gilera that Bob Brown was sitting astride,
patiently waiting for the start, (the tall
Australian had been promoted into the team
following Duke's Imola crash and had finished
third in both the 350 and 500cc TTs).

Liberati duly started on Brown's machine but the
Norton team lodged a protest. They maintained
that the move had not been sanctioned by
officials. An hour after he had won the race
Liberati was excluded and victory awarded to
veteran Jack Brett, who had ridden splendidly
on a fully streamlined Norton.

Again the Guzzi vee-eight failed, after Campbell
had set a record lap at 118.57mph, and with the
exclusion and wholesale retirement of the multis,
Manx Nortons took the first five places. For the
Ulster race Gilera were back at full strength and
it was in Ireland that Liberati really clinched the
title – on a course on which Duke and McIntyre
were expected to excel the courageous Italian
upset the form book by scoring a win. An Ulster
victory also clinched the 350cc title for Guzzi and
Campbell.

However, the sensation of the season was the
remarkable form of the new Mondials in the 125
and 250cc classes. These beautiful streamlined
Italian double overhead camshaft single cylinder
machines came virtually out of the blue to beat
the powerful MV effort in the small classes.

Hitherto Mondial had been a name associated
with the 125cc class, where they led the move
from two-stroke to four-stroke engines that
transformed the class from a joke to a category

Above: Belgian panorama shows Keith Campbell on a Moto
Guzzi vee-eight leading the 500cc class from team-mate
Keith Bryen with Libero Liberati (Gilera) third. The race ended
in disqualification for Liberati.
Below: one of the most effectively streamlined bikes ever used
for racing was Tarquinio Provini's 250cc Mondial of 1957.

in 1949. That year Pagani won the world
championship on one of their works machines.
With wins by Bruno Ruffo and Carlo Ubbiali, who
left MV to join them (only to return to MV!),
Mondial held the title in 1950 and 1951. After that
they rather faded away, over-awed perhaps by the
might of the NSU effort.

With NSU out and with a brilliant young rider
named Tarquinio Provini riding for them,
Mondial started the comeback trail. At Monza

Above: 125cc battle at the Belgian Grand Prix in 1958 as Romolo Ferri (Ducati) leads Carlo Ubbiali (MV), Alberto Gandossi (Ducati) and Tarquinio Provini (MV). That year 'full bin' streamlining was banned.
Below: challenger in the 250cc class in 1958 and 1959 was the twin-cylinder two-stroke East German MZ.

in 1956 Provini only failed to beat Ubbiali (MV) in the 125cc class by a split second – and this was only a sign of brilliant things to come.

During the winter Mondial built completely new 125cc and 250cc mounts for Provini and newly-signed team members Cecil Sandford and Sammy Miller (the same Miller who was to become the world's finest trials rider). The engines were straightforward double overhead camshaft singles, the smaller giving about 18bhp

at 12,000rpm and the larger unit (very much over-square at 75×56.4mm) around 30bhp at 10,800rpm. A novelty at the time was that both were fitted with seven-speed gearboxes. Both were very comprehensively streamlined – in fact the works Mondials of 1957 were probably the best streamlined machines ever used in world championship racing.

Provini cleaned up in the 125cc championship while Sandford won the 250cc class, where Provini took second place. Miller came within an ace of winning the bigger class at the TT, coming off on the last corner when leading and pushing home to finish fifth.

Then came the crunch. Gilera, Guzzi and Mondial jointly announced their withdrawal from racing. The Italian factories had followed the trend started in 1954 by Norton, AJS and NSU and in the intervening years by DKW. At first the works riders could not believe it – and neither could the race fans. Racing without famous names like Gilera and Guzzi was unthinkable.

At the same time the FIM acted to restrict the use of streamlining. The 'full-bin' types were forbidden and fairings were restricted so that they no longer enclosed the front wheel or the rider. Within a matter of weeks the whole racing scene had changed.

For a while MV hovered on the brink. Then Count Domenico Agusta decided to continue works support for racing. This helped tremendously, but the following three years were a 'dark age' in the history of the sport. MV won all

four solo titles in 1958, 1959 and 1960, for there was little real opposition despite gallant attempts by Ducati in the 125cc class, Morini and CZ (with a four-stroke) in the 250cc class, and Jawa in the 350cc class.

The only exception to the Italian domination came in the two lightweight classes when the two-stroke East German MZs appeared. DKW had tried to keep the two-stroke flag flying with their three-cylinder 350cc (they also raced a single cylinder 125cc and a twin 250cc occasionally) but they had never been able to beat the best of the four strokes. Now MZ came up with a completely new type of two-stroke. The secret of their success, discovered by a technical team led by Walter Kaaden, was to harness pulse waves in the exhaust system to aid both cylinder filling and the extraction of exhaust gases. This system

Hailwood arrives! Aged just 18, Mike Hailwood (*right*) joins MV aces Provini and Ubbiali in the winner's enclosure after the 250cc TT. He finished third on his NSU.
Below: Rhodesian Gary Hocking went so fast on the works 250cc MZ two-stroke that the MV Agusta factory signed him in 1960. Here Hocking wins the 1959 Ulster on an MZ.

A cloud of smoke and John Surtees (MV) gets away at the start of the 1958 Senior TT on the Isle of Man. Surtees won the race by over five minutes!

works in much the same way as a megaphone exhaust system on a four stroke. MZ developed this discovery, using the expansion chambers which became standard wear on all racing two-strokes, in conjunction with a disc valve to control the induction.

The result was a startling increase in power that put the unfashionable two-stroke right back in the racing business – and this trend, started in the MZ factory amid pine forests at Zschopau in East Germany (home of the original DKW factory) has continued until now two-strokes rule the roost not only in the lightweight classes but in the 350 and 500 divisions too, except for

stubborn and effective resistance by MV!

MZ first hit the racing headlines in 1958 when Fugner on the twin-cylinder 250cc model won his class at the Swedish Grand Prix. Next year MZ lent a works two-fifty to brilliant Rhodesian Gary Hocking. He responded by winning the class at both the Swedish and Ulster. Faced with losing the championship MV moved in and 'bought' Hocking. They offered him a works contract for 1960 and with the East Germans unable or unwilling to match the terms Hocking signed for the Italian factory.

That same year came the first sign of a move that revolutionised racing even more than the advent of the new type of two-stroke, although the two developments are inextricably interwoven. This was the first appearance of the Japanese on the European scene.

JAPANESE INVASION

Japanese bikes at the TT! The imagination of enthusiasts boggled. No one in Europe knew much about the fast growing Japanese motorcycle industry. What would the bikes be like?

Honda pioneered the Oriental invasion in 1959 when they contested only the TT, and only the 125cc class, with machines that looked like scaled-down versions of the 250cc NSU which had been retired from active service five years earlier. Like the NSUs, they were beautifully made machines, which followed orthodox lines.

Double overhead camshafts were shaft driven and the twin-cylinder 44 × 41mm engine revved to 14,000rpm, producing 18.5bhp. Honda relied on Japanese riders and their team was no match for the contemporary MV, Ducati and MZ machines; the Honda team returned to Japan immediately after the TT.

First glimpse that European race fans had of the Japanese was when Honda sent a team to contest the 125cc class of the 1959 TT. Here a rider returns after practice.

They had learned a lot – and they were back in Europe in 1960 with a completely new 125cc twin and an impressive 250cc four, which demonstrated that the Japanese company was not content just to copy European designs. They had also learned their lesson about riders and like the Italian teams of a decade earlier they 'bought in' talent to race their machines. During the year Rhodesian Jim Redman and Australians Tom Phillis and Bob Brown raced the bigger Hondas (Brown unfortunately lost his life when he crashed in the German Grand Prix at Solitude).

Still Honda were beaten. Their 1960 machines were promising but no match for the works MVs. Ubbiali clinched the lightweight championships to bring his tally of titles to nine – a record broken only by Agostini. But at the end of the year he was forced into retirement. MV decided to quit the smaller classes and they restricted their activities in the bigger divisions to sponsoring Gary Hocking.

Would Honda have triumphed so convincingly in 1961 if MV had kept on racing? It is a question no one can answer. The graph of Honda effort and success was rising rapidly while the MV effort was flagging as sales of motor-cycles in Italy took a disastrous dive. Certainly it would have needed a tremendous effort by the Italian factory to stem the Honda tide, for in 1961 the Japanese factory flooded the classics with works machines.

In addition to fielding Phillis and Redman on factory machines they signed Luigi Taveri from

MV and loaned bikes to a bright young star named Mike Hailwood and to Bob McIntyre. No wonder they overwhelmed the opposition in the 250cc class, where the four-cylinder Hondas took the first five places! Hailwood won the championship, the first of nine that this brilliant rider was to take before he switched to car racing.

The four-cylinder Honda followed the classic design pioneered by Gilera and MV with the in-line engine set across the frame but the Japanese engine had one noteworthy new feature – four valves per cylinder.

This layout had been tried in pre-war days,

notably by Rudge, but manufacturers had not persevered with it. Now it was back and the use of smaller valves and multi-cylinders meant that the Honda developed its peak power of 42–43bhp at around 13,000rpm, and could be safely revved to 14,000rpm.

In the 125cc class MZ put up a great fight with Ernst Degner level pegging with Phillis all the way through the year. The final round was in Argentina (it was at this time that the FIM started to give classic status to all sorts of odd events, regardless of suitability of circuit or the ability of organisers to finance or run a world

At the end of the 1963 season Phil Read joined Yamaha to race their new 250cc RD56 twin. It proved a wise move for the following year Read won the world title, beating Jim Redman (Honda). Here Read and his mechanic relax with cups of tea during that hectic season.

then but they were back in 1961, when they had added a two-fifty to their strength. Yamaha also appeared for the first time in Europe that year, with a team of 125cc and 250cc two-strokes led by Fumio Ito, who was already well known to European fans for his lurid efforts on a 500cc BMW during 1960.

They reaped little immediate reward. Both factories were using orthodox two-stroke engines and the works MZs were miles an hour faster. So when Degner left MZ and went to live in West Germany it was not long before Suzuki made contact with him. He spent the winter of 1961–62 working for Suzuki in Japan, and he soon proved that he had not been wasting his time for in the Spring he returned to Europe to dominate the new 50cc class. This had been granted full world championship status for 1962.

Following MZ practice the little Suzuki had a disc valve to control the induction of the single-cylinder two-stroke engine, which produced about 10bhp at 11,000rpm and gave the machine a top speed of over 90mph.

Honda had stepped up their challenge, branching into the 50cc and 350cc classes. In the smaller division they were beaten by Suzuki and the West German Kreidlers but Luigi Taveri took the 125cc title and Jim Redman won both the 250cc and 350cc championships.

So in just four seasons Japanese machines gained domination in four of the five solo classes. Only in the 500cc division did a European machine triumph–thanks to MV Agusta, who had signed Hailwood to team with Rhodesian Gary Hocking, who had won the 350 and 500cc titles for the Italian factory in 1961.

Highlight of the 1962 season was the battle for 350cc honours between the new Hondas, enlarged versions of their successful 250cc four-cylinder design, and the old and heavy MV Agustas, scaled down versions of the Italian factory's five-hundreds.

The new Hondas (with 49 × 45mm bore/stroke engines which had a power output of over 50bhp at 12,500rpm) made a tragic debut in the TT, when Tom Phillis crashed and was fatally injured. The race was won by Hailwood from Hocking, but the Rhodesian was so upset by the death of Phillis that after winning the 500cc TT he quit the sport.

championship event) and just before the race Degner decided to defect from East Germany. He left the team while they were in Sweden for the Grand Prix and went to live in West Germany.

At the time he was actually leading the championship and in an effort to clinch it he borrowed an EMC from Joe Ehrlich. This machine was very similar to the MZ except that it was water-cooled. Unfortunately for Degner it failed in South America and Phillis took the title.

Suzuki had followed the Honda lead and had sent a works team to contest the 125cc TT in 1960. Their little two-strokes had been outpaced

Ironically he lost his life in a car racing accident within a year.

Following the TT Redman won four events in succession to clinch the title. Hailwood had a clear run in the 500cc class and that year he also raced Joe Ehrlich's British-built water-cooled 125cc racer, finishing fifth in the championship and very nearly winning the class at the Spanish Grand Prix, where a split exhaust system sapped the power towards the end and dropped him to fourth place.

The championship battles became more intense in 1963 with Suzuki holding their 50cc title, New Zealander Hugh Anderson beating Kreidler ace Hans-Georg Anscheidt after a season-long battle, and successfully dislodging Honda from the top of the 125cc tree.

Their bike for this class was again a Degner-inspired design, with a disc valve air-cooled twin cylinder engine. With it Anderson soundly thrashed the Hondas, winning six world championship races – the calendar of events by now having escalated from the original six to an unwieldy twelve.

Honda in fact were finding the going tough and in the 250cc class they got a fright when Provini, now racing for Morini, took Redman to the final round and lost the title to him by only two points.

The Morini was a single-cylinder four-stoke, and this near-success for the Italian factory proved that multi-cylinder engines were by no means essential.

At last Yamaha were getting somewhere too. Following the MZ disc-valve trail they had abandoned their orthodox two-stroke and had returned to the fray with a very competitive air-cooled disc-valve twin. Fumio Ito won the class in Belgium and finished third in the championship.

Redman again got the better of Hailwood and MV Agusta in the 350cc class and 500cc racing was given a lift by the reappearance of Gilera. Their machines had been 'mothballed' at the end of 1957 and were wheeled out for the 1963 season when they were raced under the 'Scuderia Duke'

Below, left: Mike Hailwood scored the first of his nine world championship successes on a 250cc four-cylinder Honda in 1961. Here he is seen in action during the French Grand Prix at Clermont-Ferrand.
Below: Ernst Degner on a works 250cc MZ leads Australian Tom Phillis (Honda) during the 1961 Austrian Grand Prix. Degner, then living in East Germany, won the race by half a wheel! These two fought it out in the 125cc championship, too, but at the end of the year Degner left East Germany and MZ and lost his chance of the title.

50

banner, Geoff Duke managing the team for the factory.

Five seasons is a long time to be out of racing and the return proved something of a disaster. John Hartle, Phil Read and Derek Minter were signed to race the bikes but they simply could not match Hailwood and his MV Agusta, and the only race they won was the Dutch TT when Mike dropped out. Hailwood finished the year as champion and the final blow for Gilera came when Alan Shepherd outscored them with a Matchless to take second place, a point ahead of Hartle. At the end of 1963 Read joined the Yamaha team as Gilera faded from the scene.

The stage was now set for a flat out struggle for power involving the three Japanese giants, Yamaha, Honda and Suzuki.

Right: a quiet moment in the Honda camp as Jim Redman (*left*) discusses the situation with team-mate Luigi Taveri of Switzerland. These two aces were the mainstays of the Honda challenge in the early 1960s and between them won nine world championships for the Japanese factory. Both retired wealthy men.
Below: one of the hardest triers in the sport was John Hartle, seen here on one of the Scuderia Duke 500cc four-cylinder Gileras during the 1963 season. Hartle raced works bikes for Norton, MV and Gilera.

THE RACE FOR CYLINDERS

The 1964 season ushered in another 'golden age' of racing. It was to last three years and during that period more exotic new racing machines appeared on the circuits than at any time in the history of the sport. The main contestants were Honda, who for policy reasons raced four-strokes, and Yamaha and Suzuki, who by this time had developed really competitive two-strokes using the disc valve and expansion chamber arrangement invented and developed by MZ in East Germany.

Honda faced a crisis. The only way that they could combat the rising tide of the two strokes was to increase the efficiency of their engines by increasing the number of cylinders. This they did to such brilliant effect that Yamaha and Suzuki were forced to reply in kind – by designing and developing complex multi-cylinder two-stroke engines. The costs of these programmes were enormous.

During 1964 Honda replaced their single-cylinder 50cc racer with a twin; their twin-cylinder 125cc with a four-cylinder; their four-cylinder 250cc with a fantastic in-line six mounted across the frame, and the successful 350cc four with a redesigned model with the same number of cylinders.

Facts and figures can be dull, but the statistics of these new Hondas are eye-opening even today. The 50cc twin with tiny cylinders (33×29.2mm) broke all previous records for a racing engine by peaking at 19,700rpm, and they were in fact taken to over 20,000rpm by their riders. Gear ratios had been increased to ten and the engines gave 13bhp, enough to propel the little Honda at over 100mph.

The 125cc four-cylinder (35×32mm) revved to 16,000, produced 25bhp, had an eight-speed gearbox and topped 120mph. Both these models were ready for the start of the year, but the six-cylinder 250cc was not introduced until the end of the season, in an effort to counter the successful twin-cylinder RD56 Yamahas. This six-cylinder Honda engine (39×34.5mm) screamed out 53bhp at 16,500rpm, and drove through an eight-speed gearbox. The machine was good for close to 150mph.

These were incredible machines produced at incredible expense – yet they were not good enough to stem the two-stroke tide. In the 50cc class New Zealander Hugh Anderson (Suzuki) finished the year as world champion and in the important 250cc class Phil Read riding the relatively 'old fashioned' twin-cylinder Yamaha was the champion.

Honda had the consolation of ousting Suzuki from the top of the 125cc table with Luigi Taveri winning the championship and in the 350cc division they had things all their own way, Redman coasting to his third championship in succession.

In 1965 Honda got the upper hand in the 50cc class, with Ulster's Ralph Bryans winning the

Above: for the 1965 season MV Agusta produced a brand new engine, a three cylinder double-overhead camshaft unit. It started life as a 350cc but in 1966 a 500cc engine was developed. The picture shows the 1972 version of the 500cc unit. Using engines of this type Giacomo Agostini scored his record breaking run of twelve world championships.
Left: Switzerland's Fritz Scheidegger and his English passenger John Robinson broke the German hold on the sidecar world championships, winning the title in 1965 and again in 1966.

Above: highlight of the 1964 season was the struggle for 250cc championship honours between Jim Redman (Honda) and Phil Read (Yamaha). Here Redman leads at the West German Grand Prix but Read took the title. The bike that carried Read to victory that year was the RD56 Yamaha (*left*). The engine was an air-cooled, twin-cylinder two-stroke with disc valves. It produced 55–56bhp, revved to 12,000rpm and drove via a seven-speed gearbox.

title from team mate Taveri, who pushed Anderson down to third place. But Suzuki hit back to regain the 125cc crown, Anderson proving invincible on a redesigned water-cooled, disc-valve Suzuki twin. The four-cylinder Hondas were completely outpaced and were replaced at the end of the year by a five-cylinder model!

This fantastic little machine (33 × 29.2mm) was literally two and a half 50cc engines joined end to end. The first models revved to 18,000rpm and produced 30bhp, but later versions went to over 20,000rpm and gave close to 35bhp.

Opposite: four, five and six cylinder Hondas!
Top: The four cylinder 125cc Honda was introduced in 1964. Bore and stroke dimensions were 35 × 32mm and revved to 16,000. It had an eight speed gearbox and was capable of 125mph.
Opposite, centre: the 125cc Honda four was not fast enough — and in 1965 was replaced by the five-cylinder model shown here. There were two exhaust pipes each side with the fifth one curving round and coming out high-level under the rider's right thigh. Later models revved to 20,000rpm!
Opposite: Honda's most successful design was the six-cylinder. This first appeared in 1964 as a 250cc but a 350cc version was added. Hailwood scored many victories on these sixes.

Read and Yamaha continued on their winning way in the 250cc class, where the RD56 twin (56 × 50.7mm) was by this time giving over 50bhp at 13,000rpm, and the machine scoring heavily over the Honda when it came to weight. Even in the 350cc class Honda did not have things all their own way. For MV Agusta were back with a new machine and a new rider.

The Italian factory had taken a novel line. Instead of adding cylinders they developed a brand new three-cylinder racer to replace the massive four, relying on better handling, a smaller frontal area and lightness to offset the possible extra power of their rivals.

The new rider was Giacomo Agostini. The eldest son of wealthy Italian parents, he had started racing in hill-climbs and had made his name racing a two-fifty for the Morini factory.

MV Agusta and Agostini shook Honda by almost snatching the world championship from them, a broken contact breaker spring eliminating Agostini from the final round (the Japanese Grand Prix) when he was holding a commanding

lead. Team-mate Hailwood won the race on the second MV Agusta in the event, a humbling experience for Honda in front of their own crowd.

Honda responded by buying Hailwood! It was a trick that MV had used in the past, notably when they signed Gary Hocking during the 1959 season just when it looked as though the Rhodesian might snatch the 250cc title for MZ. So the Italians could hardly complain.

At the same time Honda decided to contest all five solo classes in 1966, adding a 500cc four-cylinder model to their line up and replacing the threatened 350cc 'four' with an enlarged version of the six-cylinder 250cc machine. The capacity was increased to 296cc (41 × 37.5mm) and with an 11 to 1 compression ratio (100 octane fuel had long since replaced the 72 octane of the immediate post-war years) this 'six' developed about 65bhp and revved to 17,000rpm.

The 250cc six-cylinder, 125cc five-cylinder, and 50cc twin machines were retained. Honda won all five manufacturers championships that year but they suffered two defeats in the individual championships, the ones that gain publicity. In the 50cc class Hans-Georg Anscheidt, who had switched from Kreidler to Suzuki the previous year, took the title.

Yamaha had taken over as the main challengers in the 125cc division. They had replaced their earlier air-cooled twin with a water-cooled model

Left: the world's greatest 'do-it-yourself' grandstand builders live in East Germany. Year after year they erect these incredible vantage points to get a better view of the East German Grand Prix at the Sachsenring.
Below: a rare shot of Mike Hailwood on a 350cc three cylinder MV. He raced this bike a few times in 1965.

and on it Bill Ivy finished second, beaten by Taveri (Honda). For the 250cc class Yamaha had decided to replace the very successful air-cooled twin-cylinder RD56 model with a complex water cooled, four-cylinder machine, which was first raced by Read in the Italian GP at the end of 1965. To retain the disc valves the engine was a vee-four, one 125cc twin atop another with the crankshafts geared together.

The 1966 model was a massive machine and naturally enough there were teething troubles. It took Read all year to sort out the handling and

it was not a match for the Honda until a modified version was developed for the following season. With Yamaha busy working on this new racer, Hailwood and Honda dominated the class with 'Mike the Bike' taking the title by winning the first eight 250cc races in the championship.

The relatively inexperienced Agostini gave Hailwood a run for his money in the 350cc class, actually scoring the same gross number of points (48 apiece), but with each man's six best scores counting Hailwood took the title by 48 to 42.

It was in the 500cc class that Honda suffered

Right: Giacomo Agostini joined MV Agusta from Morini early in 1965 and this photograph of him astride the then new 350cc three-cylinder racer was taken in March that year. Since then this Italian partnership has dominated the big classes of world championship road racing.
Below: Mike Hailwood flat-out on the 500cc MV Agusta at the Dutch TT in 1965. The British ace won the 500cc title four years in succession on Italian bikes.

the heaviest blow. The big capacity machines have always carried more prestige than any other and when Honda signed Hailwood and stepped up into the class for the first time few expected anything but a clean sweep for the Japanese factory. The bike, however, proved disappointing. It was a massive four-cylinder of the type raced by Gilera and MV Agusta for well over a decade. There was nothing new or clever about it, and it proved an inferior grand prix machine to the new three-cylinder MV Agusta, developed from the factory's 350cc model.

Yet the brilliance of Hailwood might still have carried off the individual honours had it not been for politics. Jim Redman, for several years captain of the Honda team, insisted that he be allowed to win the championship. He planned to retire and wanted to leave motor cycling with the 500cc title. In return he was prepared to concede the 250 and 350cc championships to Hailwood.

New-boy in the team Hailwood had little option but to agree. He was a close friend of Redman and despite the fact that he had set a record by winning the 500cc title on an MV four years in

Left: New Zealander Hugh Anderson won four titles for Suzuki. Here he fights it out with Phil Read (Yamaha) in the 125cc class of the Dutch TT in 1965.
Below: the 125 water-cooled twin-cylinder Yamaha was first raced in 1965 and was in fact a mobile test-bed for the complicated vee-four 250cc racer that the Japanese factory was developing. Because of this it was never raced for a full season, but Phil Read won the 1965 125cc TT on one and Bill Ivy scored with these models in 1966.

Above: Canadian Mike Duff grins as he and his helpers work on the factory RD56 Yamaha which he rode so brilliantly during the 1965 season. A badly broken leg at the Japanese Grand Prix at the end of the year virtually finished his racing career.

Opposite, top: if in the mid 1960s Mike Hailwood could not borrow a works MV from the factory he would sometimes turn out on a borrowed bike for a British meeting. Here he waves a foot as he sits astride a Syd Mularney Norton at Brands. Alongside him is Bill Ivy on Geoff Ward's Monard.

Right: damp day at the Nürburgring as the 350cc starters in the 1965 West German Grand Prix get away. The race was won by Agostini. The majority of riders hate the rain. It makes racing a grim, cold and sodden business.

Hero of the 1966 season was Giacomo Agostini, who despite his inexperience rode works MVs brilliantly to beat the Honda challenge in the 500cc class. Here he leads Redman.

succession (1962–65) he agreed. Redman started well by winning in West Germany (Hockenheim) and in Holland, with Agostini second in both races. There was only one big Honda available for the first event so Hailwood was a non-starter. In Holland the mechanics concentrated their efforts on getting Redman's machine right. They managed this – at the expense of Hailwood, whose bike developed gearbox trouble and eventually threw him off when he missed a gear.

For the Belgian GP Agostini had to rely on one of the old four-cylinder MV Agustas. His new 'three' had given trouble. It looked as though Honda must go further ahead. Then the elements took a hand. It poured with rain. Redman came off his Honda at high speed, injured his shoulder and never raced for the Japanese factory again. Agostini kept doggedly on to win – and to take the

lead in the championship table from Redman. With the Rhodesian out it was up to Hailwood – but Mike had not scored a single championship point.

Agostini looked set to increase his advantage when he built up a winning lead in East Germany after Hailwood had retired. But a 130mph crash put the Italian out of that race and left him far from fit for the Czech GP, run the following weekend. Hailwood siezed his chance and won in Czechoslovakia, with Agostini second. The Italian turned the tables to score in Finland, only to be beaten by Hailwood at the Ulster GP and in the TT, delayed that year until September because of a seamen's strike.

The title was decided at the Italian GP at Monza. There the Honda's gearbox failed and Agostini won unchallenged to take the 500cc world championship. The young challenger had upset the form book by beating Hailwood and Honda, helped by the team politics that had handicapped Hailwood during the early races.

ORIENTAL EFFORT FADES

The Honda challenge was flagging. It had cost the Japanese company several hundred thousand pounds to develop their four, five and six cylinder racers but despite their ingenuity the two-strokes kept coming back at them. Yamaha were close to perfecting their four-cylinder 250cc and had a similar 125cc model on the way. The latest twin-cylinder water-cooled 50cc Suzuki was more than a match for the tiny Honda – and both companies were pouring money into developing three-cylinder 50cc racers!

As costs spiralled so the benefits of winning races in Europe dwindled. The motor-cycle market had collapsed. Now America was the place to sell motor-cycles. After a long hard look at the situation Honda made their decision. They pulled out of the 50cc and 125cc classes completely but agreed to give Hailwood and Ralph Bryans limited factory support to race existing works machines in the three bigger classes.

The scene was set for 1967. Like Honda the Suzuki effort was fading. Only Yamaha stepped up the challenge and again it was the 250cc class which produced the closest finish as Hailwood on a six-cylinder Honda fought it out with Read and Ivy on the improved, lower and lighter Yamaha fours. It was so close that even after the final round in Japan few were certain who had won.

Both men finished with 50 points but Hailwood had five wins to Read's four. This was enough to give him the title. Yamaha gained some consolation in the 125cc class with little Bill Ivy taking the title ahead of Read and Stuart Graham, son of 1949 500cc champion Les, who had switched to

In 1966 and 1967 Mike Hailwood (Honda) and Phil Read (Yamaha) fought out a series of great battles in the 250cc class, but in both years Hailwood won the championship. This sequence from the 1967 Ulster Grand Prix catches a highlight of one of those chases.
Top: Read is off at the hairpin and Hailwood aims for the gap between Phil and the straw bales.
Centre: he just makes it as Read struggles to pick the Yamaha up.
Right: Mike gets away as the Yamaha rider prepares to remount.

Left: Agostini after winning the 1972 Senior TT.
Far left, top: the placed men after the 1972 350cc Swedish GP. From the left: Saarinen, Agostini and Read; centre: Chas Mortimer (Yamaha) leads Borje Jansson (Maico) during the 1972 125cc Swedish GP; bottom: a champion and his machine – Finland's Jarno Saarinen prepares his 250cc Yamaha for the 1972 Swedish GP.

In 1967 Giacomo Agostini (MV) and Mike Hailwood (Honda) battled it out in the 500cc class. Above: Agostini leads at the Dutch TT; Hailwood got ahead to win the race. Right: the Senior TT that year was reckoned by many to be the best ever. After three laps the two aces pit-stopped together. Hailwood (nearest) gets away first.

Suzuki from Honda. Suzuki picked up the 50cc title but this was a hollow victory for they alone used multi-cylinder works bikes with Anscheidt winning from Yoshima Katayama and Graham.

In the 350cc class Hailwood and the six-cylinder Honda were just too good for Agostini and MV Agusta but the 500cc championship again saw a great duel between these aces. Probably the most exciting race of the series was the Senior TT in the Isle of Man. Both riders were on great form and the lap record was smashed time and again. Both men lapped at over 108mph and Agostini was just two seconds ahead on the fifth lap of the seven lap race when the rear chain on the MV Agusta jumped the sprockets and broke.

Hailwood went on to win, but he cursed the poor handling of the massive Honda and freely admitted that but for that chain trouble Agostini would probably have won. For some reason the Honda would not go in a straight line – even on the straights it weaved from side to side, and Hailwood had to fight it every inch of the way.

Through the speed trap at the Highlander on one of the fastest parts of the 37.7 mile circuit (organised by the journal *Motor Cycle* and manned by officials of the National Sprint Association using electronic gear) the Honda clocked 154.5mph, fractionally faster than the MV.

Agostini hit back and at the end of the year tied with Hailwood with 46 points each. But this time Hailwood did not have more wins – both had scored five victories. A tie on wins is broken by the number of second places each man has scored – and Agostini retained his title having three second places to Hailwood's two. It could not have been much closer.

Suzuki, whose experiments with a four-cylinder 250cc machine had been unsuccessful,

Left: in 1967 the little four-cylinder water-cooled 125cc Yamahas were unbeatable. Here Bill Ivy leads team-mate Phil Read at the Ulster Grand Prix while Stuart Graham (Suzuki) does his best to stay with them.
Left, below: out of racing for several years following a serious accident, Helmut Fath returned to the scene in 1967 with the four-cylinder Urs. Here Fath (*left*) works on the machine at the West German Grand Prix in 1967.
Below: when Yamaha pulled out Bill Ivy switched to a works four-cylinder Jawa for the 350cc class. Here Ivy (*right*) nips inside Agostini (MV) at the 1969 Dutch TT.

unveiled a new four cylinder 125cc bike for the Japanese GP in 1967, and Graham rode it to second place. It was the only time the bike was ever raced for that winter Suzuki quit world championship racing, although following the Honda example they let 50cc world champion Anscheidt defend his title the next year on one of their existing works machines.

Honda cut back even further. They expressly forbade Hailwood and Bryans to ride in world championship races. Both men had to look after their machines themselves and they could use them only in non-title races. The battle of the giants that had raged in all five solo classes and which faltered when Honda had pulled out of the lightweight classes before the 1967 season was finally at an end.

Yamaha decided to soldier on in 1968 and a bitter rivalry that developed between Phil Read and Bill Ivy did much to liven up what would otherwise have been a dull year. Despite his great efforts during four seasons Read was out of favour with Yamaha, who now regarded Ivy as their number one. They decided that he should win both 125cc and 250cc world championships. Read was far from happy and eventually it was agreed that Ivy would be number one for the 250cc class while Read would take the 125cc championship.

It was an uneasy truce. Each man was out to

prove himself the better rider and as the season wore on the feud got more obvious and bitter. At the TT Ivy set a fantastic pace in the 125cc race, smashing the lap record and clocking the first ever 100mph lap on a 125cc machine – a record no rider was to approach during the next five years. On the last lap he stopped to let Read pass him and win. Ivy had set out to make it obvious that he was the better rider yet he led Read by only a few seconds despite the fact that Ivy's smaller build and lighter weight made him a more suitable jockey for a 125cc machine.

Fate played into Read's hands. He clinched the 125cc title by mid-season. Now he could concentrate on the 250cc class and it was difficult for Yamaha to do anything about it. They were warned by the FIM that riders must be free to try and win any race in which they competed. Not to do so amounted to conduct prejudicial to the sport and could end in suspension.

Yamaha dithered. They could have taken Read's machine away from him and given Ivy a clear run. But this would have stirred up bad publicity and when the situation was boiled down to essentials did it really matter to them who won the titles as long as they were riding Yamaha machines? So Yamaha let their two bickering team-mates get on with it. Eventually they tied with 52 points. Both had five wins and two

second places. The tie was resolved by the total times of the races they had both completed – and Read was champion.

In the sidecar class there was a sensation – a BMW did not win! Ever since Wilhelm Noll beat Eric Oliver (Norton) to take the title in 1954 outfits powered by the Munich-built horizontally opposed twin-cylinder engines had won the title. When factory support faded in the late 1950s these engines had been built into specials and Helmut Fath, Max Deubel, Fritz Scheidegger and Klaus Enders had all won the title on home-built outfits, using engines built and maintained by themselves or by private tuners, although all got some assistance from BMW at one time or another.

Fath, who won the title on a BMW in 1960, was seriously injured in a racing accident in 1961. He was out of the sport for five years and during that time, with the help of West German friends, he designed, built and developed a four-cylinder engine. It was a double overhead camshaft unit with fuel injection and they named it the Urs – the first three letters of Ursenbach, the town near Fath's home.

In 1967 Fath made his comeback and his home-made bike was good enough to win the title – to take the championship from BMW. But he lost it again in 1969 when he crashed while competing

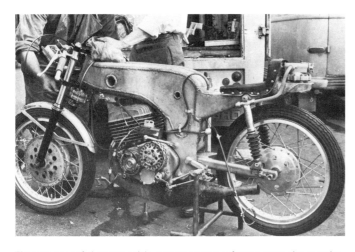

First successful racer with a monocoque frame was the works 250cc Ossa raced by Santiago Herrero. This is the 1969 model. The welded alloy frame serves also as a fuel tank.

Vital moments from the 250cc championship in 1969 and 1970.
Left, below: Australian Kel Carruthers clinches the title on a works Benelli at the Yugoslav GP in 1969.
Below: Rod Gould (Yamaha) leads Phil Read (Yamaha) and Carruthers (Yamaha) in the vital round, the Italian GP. Gould won the race to take the title from Carruthers who finished second.

in a non-championship event in Finland and Enders narrowly beat him for the title 60 points to 55.

By 1969 the Japanese factories had completely faded from the scene and the only support from the orient took the form of a factory machine that Kawasaki, a name new to Europe, lent to Dave Simmonds for the 125cc class, and the new and very competitive TD2 250cc and TR2 350cc Yamahas which had just come on the market via America. They had in fact been developed by Yamaha for American racing and the prototype models had appeared at Daytona. Now Yamaha made a batch and Europe was reaping the benefit. For the first time for many years a rider could buy a machine which gave him a chance of finishing among the leaders.

These Yamaha racers were absurdly simple two-stroke twins. No disc valves, no complications. They relied for their performance on a new style of porting developed by Yamaha and known as the five port system. Each cylinder had four transfer ports and one exhaust port, with the inlets arranged to give maximum efficiency at high revs when they worked in conjunction with the all-important expansion chamber exhaust system. The smaller engine gave about 42–44bhp at 10,000rpm and the larger 52–54bhp at 9,500rpm.

The machines were so much better than any

other available that within a year the majority
of the fields in both classes were Yamaha
mounted. Despite this it was a relatively quiet
year with Agostini cruising to easy successes in
two big classes and Simmonds on the Kawasaki
out in front in the majority of 125cc events.

Only in the 50cc and 250cc classes were the
championships close fought. After a year-long
struggle Spaniard Angel Nieto riding a Spanish
Derbi took the 50cc class by a single point from
Dutchman Aalt Toersen on a West German
Kreidler. For the first time the FIM had imposed
restrictions – 50cc machines could only be
powered by single cylinder engines and a
maximum of six speeds was the limit. This did not
affect the Japanese manufacturers, who had quit
the scene by the time the restrictions were
imposed.

The 250cc class, living up to its reputation, saw
a real cliff-hanger and the outcome was not
decided until the final round, the Yugoslav
Grand Prix run on a tricky sea-front circuit at
Opatija, an Adriatic resort. There Kel Carruthers
won the race on a four cylinder works Benelli
from team-mate Gilberto Parlotti. Challenger
Santiago Herrero who had battled with the
Benellis throughout the season on the incredibly
fast single cylinder two-stroke Spanish Ossa with
its unique monocoque frame of welded alloy,
crashed and lost his chance, although he was not
seriously hurt. Riding one of the new Yamahas
Sweden's Kent Andersson took advantage of

Photographers crowd in close to the circuit at the 1971 Dutch
TT – the one on the right seems to be taking a nap! Every
year since the war the Dutch classic has attracted over
100,000 spectators, and it is the biggest sporting event of the
year in Holland.

Herrero's bad luck to finish second in the
championship.

The 350cc class might have been close fought,
too, if Bill Ivy's partnership with the Czech Jawa
factory had not ended tragically at the East
German Grand Prix. Jawa had been racing a four
cylinder two-stroke without success for two
seasons and when Yamaha pulled out they signed
Ivy to race the machine in world championship
events – an arrangement which suited Bill because
it provided funds for his car racing programme.
He had one brilliant race, in the Dutch TT where
he caught and passed Agostini before the Jawa
gave trouble and he dropped back to finish second.
Then during a wet practice session in East
Germany the temperamental Jawa seized up, and
Ivy lost his life in the ensuing crash.

For 1970 the FIM introduced more restrictions.
Both 125 and 250cc machines were limited to twin-
cylinders and six-speed gearboxes. The only people
affected were Benelli who had to pension off their
four-cylinder machines. The idea behind these
limitations was to rule out exotic multis of the
type that had cost the Japanese factories so much
money, and which had eventually caused them to
pull out of the sport. By restricting the number of

Spaniard Angel Nieto is the star of the lightweight riders. Competing on Spanish-built Derbi two-strokes this little ace from Madrid won five world titles in four seasons and completed the 50cc and 125cc double in 1972. Here he is seen in action on his 50cc mount at the 1970 Dutch TT.

cylinders and gear ratios the FIM hoped to encourage the smaller manufacturers back into racing, where the withdrawal of Honda (whose 1966 50cc was a double overhead camshaft twin with a 10 speed gearbox) had left only Suzuki (two-stroke twin with 12 or 14 speed gearboxes). They too faded from the scene leaving only Anscheidt to win the 1968 title before the restrictions were imposed.

In fact the FIM had originally intended to bring the restrictions into force in 1970 but when only Anscheidt was left they accelerated the legislation by a year. This encouraged Derbi, Kreidler (via their Dutch agent van Veen who financed the team himself) and the small Dutch Jamathi concern to support the 50cc class in 1969, when all three fielded teams.

As far as the 250cc category was concerned the restrictions played straight into the hands of Yamaha. The TD2 was far and away the most competitive racer that could be bought and with the elimination of the factory four-cylinder Benellis (which had been hard pressed to beat the best of the Yamahas) the Japanese two-strokes were left as top dogs, with Santiago Herrero and the lone Ossa as the only really serious threat.

The Spaniard started the season well but lost his life when he crashed in the TT.

Rod Gould went on to win the race and the championship, outscoring Kel Carruthers who had switched from a works Benelli to a Yamaha to defend his title. This Japanese factory had come back into the sport in a limited way, and were backing Gould and Andersson with free machines and spares plus a small financial grant. This was nothing like the massive support that they had given their works riders a few years before, but it was better than nothing. The bikes Gould and Andersson rode were normal production racing Yamahas, but they sometimes tried out experimental components for the factory.

Carruthers, despite the fact that he was the reigning champion, was not invited to join the team and neither was Phil Read who had won four championships for Yamaha. Carruthers in fact rode for American Don Vesco. This tie-up was arranged by Gould, who must have wondered if he had done the right thing when his Australian rival pressed him hard during the early part of the season!

None of the championships was close fought that year. Nieto (Derbi) retained his 50cc crown winning the first four grands prix in a row. Dave Simmonds had modified his Kawasaki to suit the new formula by fitting a six-speed cluster to replace the ten-speed gearbox of the original. But he was plagued by all sorts of mechanical problems and West German Dieter Braun, riding

Off-duty moments for two of the top stars.
Above: smiling Finn Jarno Saarinen contemplates his TD2 Yamaha during a quiet moment at the 1970 Belgian G.P.
Below: Spain's Angel Nieto follows the trend as he swops his 'pudding basin' helmet (on ground) for a full enclosure type at the 1971 Dutch TT.

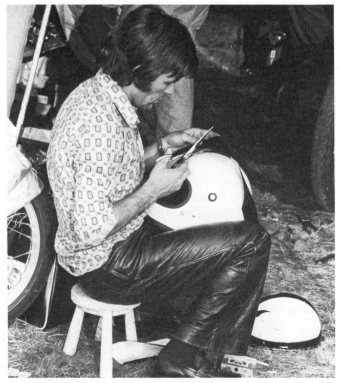

an ex-works water-cooled Suzuki twin (also with the number of gear ratios cut from 10 to 6) that he had bought from Hans Georg Anscheidt won the title. Towards the end of the season, however, Nieto on a new factory Derbi was able to beat the tall West German quite easily.

Agostini was again in a class of his own in the 350cc events with Carruthers runner-up. The Australian had started the year on a works four-cylinder Benelli but the Italian effort was half-hearted and tiring of constant frustrations he switched to a Yamaha for this class as well as for the 250cc races.

A significant trend took place in the 500cc class in 1970. Until then 500cc racing had been dominated by four-strokes, with the famous Manx Norton and G50 Matchless single cylinder racers forming the backbone of the class. Even when manufacture of these bikes ended, as Associated Motor Cycles went bankrupt in the early 1960s, the singles continued to do well in the hands of private owners, with Jack Findlay on his Matchless-engined special with a Bob McIntyre designed frame second in the championships in 1968 and Godfrey Nash third the following year on a very standard Manx Norton.

In fact in 1969 four-strokes of one sort of another took the top 12 places in the championship table. But the next year the two-strokes

started to infiltrate into the class. Agostini and his works three-cylinder MV Agusta were still unbeatable but the days of the four-stroke single were over. New Zealander Ginger Molloy rode one of the new three-cylinder Kawasaki HIR machines to such good effect that he finished a clear cut second and French champion Christian Ravel took seventh place on another Kawasaki. Significantly Jack Findlay, after a few races on a Seeley (an updated version of the G50 Matchless built by Colin Seeley) switched to a Suzuki twin in mid-season, while other riders increased the capacity of 350cc Yamahas and used them in the class. Most successful of these was Martti Pesonen of Finland who finished tenth in the championship.

The writing for the four-stroke was on the wall – and it was confirmed in 1971. Agostini still won as he pleased but two-strokes took the next six places in the championship and provided some good sport as Keith Turner (Suzuki), Rob Bron (Suzuki), Dave Simmonds (Kawasaki) and Jack Findlay (Suzuki) fought it out for second place. The surprise was the way in which the basically roadster twin-cylinder Suzukis put it across the production racing HIR Kawasakis.

In the 350cc class the two-stroke challenge grew to such an extent that Agostini had to ride hard to win, something he had not had to do

since Honda and Hailwood pulled out of grand prix racing at the end of 1967. Notable among his rivals was Jarno Saarinen, a Finnish university student, who rode a Yamaha for the Finnish importer. The Finn did not actually beat Agostini during 1971 but he won two grands prix and finished a good second in the table.

The fact that MV Agusta were responding to the challenge by increasing their budget was good news for racing. Unfortunately their plan to field two riders was held up when Angelo Bergamonti, signed to team with Agostini, was killed while racing in a minor meeting in Italy early in the year. He was attempting to catch Agostini in heavy rain when his machine aquaplaned. Wearing an old style crash helmet Bergamonti received head injuries from which he died. Naturally this delayed the MV Agusta plans and it was not until the end of the season that they signed Alberto Pagani, son of former Gilera and MV Agusta star Nello, as second string.

The 250cc championship in 1971 was highlighted by the return of Phil Read. Since the bitterly-fought battles of 1968 the former Yamaha star had concentrated on racing in Britain with

Man who put the sparkle into the 1972 season was 'Flying Finn' Jarno Saarinen. Here he leads the field into the first corner of the 1972 French Grand Prix at the Clermont Ferrand circuit. The race is the 350cc class and Saarinen on a water-cooled Yamaha, won it from fellow-Finn Teuvo Lansivuori (Yamaha, 62) Agostini could finish only fourth — and within a few days the three-cylinder MV had been pensioned off in favour of the new four-cylinder racer.

the occasional Continental event. Now he was back and made no secret of the fact that he was out to regain the 250cc title that he had held in 1964, 1965 and 1968. His machine was a special Yamaha that he had developed. The frame was of his own design and another notable feature was a double disc front brake. Preparation of the engines was in the hands of former sidecar world champion, Helmut Fath, the man behind the Urs four cylinder.

It proved a successful venture. Read won the

For an hour or so it looked as though Barry Sheene would be the new 125cc champion. The Londoner had ridden brilliantly throughout the year on a five year old ex-works Suzuki that he had bought from Stuart Graham, and he came to Jarama leading Nieto by 79 points to 72.

Nieto had to do well to beat him – but the Spaniard was a doubtful starter after his 50cc spill. Sheene too was in pain. He had crashed heavily the previous weekend at Mallory Park damaging his back. Luckily for Nieto the organisers had put the 125cc race last on the programme and he was sufficiently recovered to start.

During the early stages he wisely hung back, content to sit behind Sheene, Braun and Sweden's Borje Jansson, who was showing steadily improving form on a single cylinder works Maico (a disc valve, water-cooled two stroke). Braun slowed and Jansson pulled ahead. Nieto and Sheene were left to fight it out; the Spaniard had only to finish among the first four to clinch the title.

Luck played into Nieto's hands. The rear wheel of Jansson's Maico collapsed and the clutch of Sheene's Suzuki started to fail. Nieto went on to win and as he crossed the line to clinch the world championship the 30,000 crowd went mad. Led by the man with the chequered flag they rushed onto the circuit to congratulate their hero. The following riders found themselves hurtling towards a seething mass of people at well over 100mph. Several riders struck spectators and crashed but miraculously only one spectator was injured (with a broken leg). An exciting finish to the championship year.

The upsurge in racing continued during the 1972 season with the promise of a real challenge to Agostini in the 350cc class fulfilled by Jarno Saarinen who defeated the Italian world champion on several occasions during the season – the first time that anyone had done so in world championship racing since 1967. Saarinen's machine was a new water-cooled Yamaha which followed the lines of the earlier air-cooled models except that the cylinder and heads were water-cooled. This kept the engine temperature down and helped to keep power constant throughout the race. With the air-cooled models performance fell off slightly after ten minutes or so, when the engines tended to overheat and to lose the fine 'edge' of their tune.

Saarinen started brilliantly with wins in West Germany and France. MV Agusta countered by introducing a new four cylinder three-fifty and by adding Phil Read to support Agostini in this class while Pagani concentrated on 500cc racing. Not since 1960 had the Italian factory fielded so many riders or machines. Their efforts bore fruit for although Saarinen kept up the pressure and actually won more grands prix, Agostini even-

title after a close battle with Gould and Saarinen who finished the season by winning the class at the Spanish Grand Prix. Both the 50cc and 125cc championships were decided at the same event, run on the Jarama circuit near Madrid. In the 50cc race reigning champion Nieto came off his Derbi while battling with challenger Jan de Vries on a Dutch-sponsored van Veen Kreidler. He was carried away on a stretcher, while de Vries rode on to win race and title.

tually clinched the title. The vital round was the Swedish Grand Prix at Anderstorp. There Saarinen was right with Agostini until the gearbox of his Yamaha started to give trouble. The Finn dropped back and lost his chance of the championship when Read overtook him to give MV Agusta a one-two.

The 50, 125, 250 and sidecar classes were equally hard fought. In fact, none of the titles were decided until the final two rounds of the 13-round series (originally there were to have been 14 rounds, but the Ulster Grand Prix was cancelled because of the political situation in Northern Ireland). The penultimate round was the Finnish Grand Prix at the Imatra circuit close by the Russian border, where by lucky chance local hero Saarinen had the opportunity to clinch the 250cc title.

Throughout the season he had battled with Yamaha team-mate Ron Gould, a former champion, and with Italian Renzo Pasolini on the fast improving two-stroke Aermacchi, a machine very similar in design to the air-cooled Yamaha racers. Saarinen made no mistakes and to the delight of the 30,000 crowd he won the race and the championship – the first world championship to be taken by a Finn. His mount was one of the new water-cooled twin-cylinder Yamahas. These weighed only 250lb, and their engines revved to 11,000rpm and produced about 60bhp; their performance was superior to that of the famous six-cylinder Honda of 1967, and equal to that of the four-cylinder 1968 Yamaha.

Gould retired before the end of the season to take up a post as publicity manager for Yamaha in Europe, and Pasolini won the final round in Spain to finish a single point behind the Finn, who missed this race because he was racing in America.

The sidecar title was also decided in Finland.

Left: Rod Gould (Yamaha) streaks to victory in the 250cc class of the 1972 Swedish Grand Prix. It proved to be Rod's last championship win for within weeks he announced his retirement from the sport.
Below: Chris Vincent on the four-cylinder Munch leads Klaus Enders (BMW) in the 1972 Dutch TT. But Enders came through to win and later clinched his fourth world title.
Right, below: a scurry of feet and the sidecar class of the 1972 Belgian Grand Prix gets away.

West German Klaus Enders had come out of retirement after a year to try to win the championship for the fourth time. However, the new outfit built for him by Dieter Busch of Frankfurt was not ready at the start of the season and he missed the early championship rounds. Then a puncture put him out of the TT when he was leading, so he faced the tough task of having to win or finish second in all the remaining events. Riding brilliantly, the little camera mechanic from Wetzlar won the Dutch TT, the Belgian GP and the Czech GP. In Finland he had only to finish second to clinch the title. Wisely, he settled for second place, content to follow Chris Vincent, who livened up the three-wheeler scene with some brilliant riding on the four-cylinder Munch which he had taken over from 1971 champion Horst Owesle.

Owesle had been Fath's chief mechanic when the original Urs was developed. The Urs design had been sold to the West German Munch factory, and Owesle took over as its rider when Fath split with Munch. Despite his lack of experience, Owesle had won the title in 1971. But his heart was in the mechanical side and he was quite happy to retire from racing to concentrate on engine preparation when American George Bell took over the racing side of Munch for the 1972 season, and signed Vincent as the rider.

Both the 50cc and 125cc titles were still open in September, when the final round of the championship was held at Montjuich Park, Barcelona, the traditional home of the 'Spanish'. The situation was almost the same as in 1971, with Angelo Nieto in with a chance of winning both titles. Given a second chance, Nieto made no mistakes.

In the 125cc race he had only to finish among the first eight to make certain of the title and he wisely let Kent Andersson and Chas Mortimer on works Yamahas go, settling for third place and clinching the title. In the 50cc race, last in the programme and of the championship year, the situation was very different. Jan de Vries had a three point lead and Nieto had to beat him to regain the title which he had lost to the Dutch rider the previous year. In fact, the race was an anti-climax – especially for the 2,000 Dutch enthusiasts who had been ferried down in a fleet of 20 chartered aircraft – for Nieto shot away from the start and easily won from de Vries.

Only in the 500cc class did Agostini have an easy time of it and even in that class there were signs of challenge. Yamaha, who had stepped up the number of riders with factory support from two to six (retaining Gould and Andersson and adding Saarinen, Chas Mortimer, Barry Sheene and Hideo Kanaya) officially entering the class by fielding a number of three-fifty models with the engines enlarged to 354cc to make them 'legal' (under FIM rules an engine must be at least 1cc larger than the top limit of the next lower class).

The championships were over for another year, and an era ended: not a single title had been won by a British rider, and that was something which had not happened before in the 24-year history of world championship road racing.

THE CHAMPIONSHIPS

These tables cover the first 24 years of the world championship series, giving riders in each class, their nationality and the machines used, together with points gained. Where riders have scored equal numbers of points, they are placed in the order of their overall championship placings, taking into account the FIM tie-breaking methods.

When the championships were introduced in 1949 points were awarded to the first five in each race – 10 points for a win, then 8, 7, 6 and 5, plus a single point for the fastest lap, if this was set by a finisher. This system was changed in 1950, when the point for a fastest lap was abandoned and points

were awarded for the first six finishers – 8 points for a victory, then 6, 4, 3, 2 and 1 for a sixth place. This was retained until 1969, when the present method was adopted; under this a winner gains 15 points, and the other finishers 12, 10, 8, 6, 5, 4, 3, 2 and 1 down to tenth place.

Not every score counts. Under FIM rules the maximum number of rounds that count is half of the total, plus one (ignoring fractions). This means that if 12 Grands Prix are run in a particular class, a rider will count only his best 7 performances. These tables show only net points.

1949

125cc
1 N. Pagani, Italy (Mondial) 27
2 R. Magi, Italy (Morini) 14
3 U. Masetti, Italy (Morini) 13

250cc
1 B. Ruffo, Italy (Guzzi) 24
2 D. Ambrosini, Italy (Benelli) 19
3 R. Mead, GB (Mead Norton) 13

350cc
1 F. Frith, GB (Velocette) 33
2 R. Armstrong, Ireland (AJS) 18
3 A. R. Foster, GB (Velocette) 16

500cc
1 L. Graham, GB (AJS) 30
2 N. Pagani, Italy (Gilera) 29
3 A. Artesiani, Italy (Gilera) 25

Sidecar
1 E. Oliver, GB (Norton) 26
2 E. Frigerio, Italy (Gilera) 18
3 F. Vanderschrick, Belgium (Norton) 16

1950

125cc
1 B. Ruffo, Italy (Mondial) 17
2 G. Leoni, Italy (Mondial) 14
3 C. Ubbiali, Italy (Mondial) 14

250cc
1 D. Ambrosini, Italy (Benelli) 30
2 M. Cann, GB (Guzzi) 14
3 F. Anderson, GB (Guzzi) 6

350cc
1 A. R. Foster, GB (Velocette) 30
2 G. Duke, GB (Norton) 24
3 L. Graham, GB (AJS) 17

500cc
1 U. Masetti, Italy (Gilera) 28
2 G. Duke, GB (Norton) 27
3 L. Graham, GB (AJS) 17

Sidecar
1 E. Oliver, GB (Norton) 24
2 E. Frigerio, Italy (Gilera) 18
3 H. Haldemann, Switzerland (Norton) 8

1951

125cc
1 C. Ubbiali, Italy (Mondial) 20
2 G. Leoni, Italy (Mondial) 12
3 W. McCandless, Ireland (Mondial) 11

250cc
1 B. Ruffo, Italy (Guzzi) 26
2 T. L. Wood, GB (Guzzi) 21
3 D. Ambrosini, Italy (Benelli) 14

350cc
1 G. Duke, GB (Norton) 40
2 J. Lockett, GB (Norton) 19
3 W. Doran, GB (AJS) 19

500cc
1 G. Duke, GB (Norton) 35
2 Alfredo Milani, Italy (Gilera) 31
3 U. Masetti, Italy (Gilera) 21

Sidecar
1 E. Oliver, GB (Norton) 30
2 E. Frigerio, Italy (Gilera) 26
3 Albino Milani, Italy (Gilera) 19

1952

125cc
1 C. Sandford, GB (MV) 28
2 C. Ubbiali, Italy (Mondial) 24
3 E. Mendogni, Italy (Morini) 16

250cc
1 E. Lorenzetti, Italy (Guzzi) 28
2 F. Anderson, GB (Guzzi) 24
3 L. Graham, GB (Velocette) 11

350cc
1 G. Duke, GB (Norton) 32
2 R. Armstrong, Ireland (Norton) 24
3 W. R. Amm, Rhodesia (Norton) 21

500cc
1 U. Masetti, Italy (Gilera) 28
2 L. Graham, GB (MV) 25
3 R. Armstrong, Ireland (Norton) 22

Sidecar
1 C. Smith, GB (Norton) 24
2 Albino Milani, Italy (Gilera) 18
3 J. Drion, France (Norton) 17

1953

125cc
1 W. Haas, W. Germany (NSU) 30
2 C. Sandford, GB (MV) 20
3 C. Ubbiali, Italy (MV) 18

250cc
1 W. Haas, W. Germany (NSU) 28
2 R. Armstrong, Ireland (NSU) 23
3 F. Anderson, GB (Guzzi) 22

350cc
1 F. Anderson, GB (Guzzi) 30
2 E. Lorenzetti, Italy (Guzzi) 26
3 W. R. Amm, Rhodesia (Norton) 18

500cc
1 G. Duke, GB (Gilera) 38
2 R. Armstrong, Ireland (Gilera) 24
3 Alfredo Milani, Italy (Gilera) 18

Sidecar
1 E. Oliver, GB (Norton) 32
2 C. Smith, GB (Norton) 26
3 H. Haldemann, Switz. (Norton) 12

1954

125cc
1 R. Hollaus, Austria (NSU) 32
2 C. Ubbiali, Italy (MV) 18
3 H. P. Muller, W. Germany (NSU) 15

250cc
1 W. Haas, W. Germany (NSU) 32
2 R. Hollaus, Austria (NSU) 26
3 H. P. Muller, W. Germany (NSU) 17

350cc
1 F. Anderson, GB (Guzzi) 32
2 W. R. Amm, Rhodesia (Norton) 22
3 R. Coleman, New Zealand (AJS) 20

500cc
1 G. Duke, GB (Gilera) 32
2 W. R. Amm, Rhodesia (Norton) 20
3 K. Kavanagh, Australia (Norton) 16

Sidecar
1 W. Noll, W. Germany (BMW) 30
2 E. Oliver, GB (Norton) 26
3 C. Smith, GB (Norton) 22

1955

125cc
1 C.Ubbiali, Italy (MV) 32
2 L.Taveri, Switzerland (MV) 26
3 R.Venturi, Italy (MV) 16

250cc
1 H.P.Muller, W.Germany (NSU) 19
2 C.Sandford, GB (Guzzi) 14
3 W.Lomas, GB (MV) 13

350cc
1 W.Lomas, GB (Guzzi) 30
2 R.Dale, GB (Guzzi) 18
3 A.Hobl, W.Germany (DKW) 17

500cc
1 G.Duke, GB (Gilera) 32
2 R.Armstrong, Ireland (Gilera) 26
3 U.Masetti, Italy (MV) 19

Sidecar
1 W.Faust, W.Germany (BMW) 30
2 W.Noll, W.Germany (BMW) 28
3 W.Schneider, W.Germany (BMW) 22

1956

125cc
1 C.Ubbiali, Italy (MV) 32
2 R.Ferri, Italy (Gilera) 14
3 L.Taveri, Switzerland (MV) 12

250cc
1 C.Ubbiali, Italy (MV) 32
2 L.Taveri, Switzerland (MV) 26
3 E.Lorenzetti, Italy (Guzzi) 10

350cc
1 W.Lomas, GB (Guzzi) 24
2 A.Hobl, W.Germany (DKW) 17
3 R.Dale, GB (Guzzi) 17

500cc
1 J.Surtees, GB (MV) 24
2 W.Zeller, W.Germany (BMW) 16
3 J.Hartle, GB (Norton) 14

Sidecar
1 W.Noll, W.Germany (BMW) 30
2 F.Hillebrand, W.Germany (BMW) 26
3 P.V.Harris, GB (Norton) 24

1957

125cc
1 T.Provini, Italy (Mondial) 30
2 L.Taveri, Switzerland (MV) 22
3 C.Ubbiali, Italy (MV) 22

250cc
1 C.Sandford, GB (Mondial) 26
2 T.Provini, Italy (Mondial) 16
3 S.H.Miller, Ireland (Mondial) 14

350cc
1 K.Campbell, Australia (Guzzi) 30
2 R.McIntyre, Scotland (Gilera) 22
3 L.Liberati, Italy (Gilera) 22

500cc
1 L.Liberati, Italy (Gilera) 32
2 R.McIntyre, Scotland (Gilera) 20
3 J.Surtees, GB (MV) 17

Sidecar
1 F.Hillebrand, W.Germany (BMW) 28
2 W.Schneider, W.Germany (BMW) 20
3 F.Camathias, Switzerland (BMW) 17

1958

125cc
1 C.Ubbiali, Italy (MV) 32
2 A.Gandossi, Italy (Ducati) 25
3 L.Taveri, Switzerland (Ducati) 20

250cc
1 T.Provini, Italy (MV) 32
2 H.Fugner, E.Germany (MZ) 25
3 C.Ubbiali, Italy (MV) 16

350cc
1 J.Surtees, GB (MV) 32
2 J.Hartle, GB (MV) 24
3 G.Duke, GB (Norton) 17

500cc
1 J.Surtees, GB (MV) 32
2 J.Hartle, GB (MV) 20
3 R.H.Dale, GB (BMW) 13

Sidecar
1 W.Schneider, W.Germany (BMW) 30
2 F.Camathias, Switzerland (BMW) 26
3 H.Fath, W.Germany (BMW) 8

1959

125cc
1 C.Ubbiali, Italy (MV) 30
2 T.Provini, Italy (MV) 28
3 M.Hailwood, GB (Ducati) 20

250cc
1 C.Ubbiali, Italy (MV) 28
2 T.Provini, Italy (MV) 16
3 G.Hocking, Rhodesia (MZ) 16

350cc
1 J.Surtees, GB (MV) 32
2 J.Hartle, GB (MV) 16
3 R.N.Brown, Australia (Norton) 14

500cc
1 J.Surtees, GB (MV) 32
2 R.Venturi, Italy (MV) 22
3 R.N.Brown, Australia (Norton) 17

Sidecar
1 W.Schneider, W.Germany (BMW) 22
2 F.Camathias, Switzerland (BMW) 22
3 F.Scheidegger, Switzerland (BMW) 16

1960

125cc
1 C.Ubbiali, Italy (MV) 24
2 G.Hocking, Rhodesia (MV) 18
3 E.Degner, E.Germany (MZ) 16

250cc
1 C.Ubbiali, Italy (MV) 32
2 G.Hocking, Rhodesia (MV) 28
3 L.Taveri, Switzerland (MV) 11

350cc
1 J.Surtees, GB (MV) 22
2 G.Hocking, Rhodesia (MV) 22
3 J.Hartle, GB (MV/Norton) 18

500cc
1 J.Surtees, GB (MV) 32
2 R.Venturi, Italy (MV) 26
3 J.Hartle, GB (Norton/MV) 16

Sidecar
1 H.Fath, W.Germany (BMW) 24
2 F.Scheidegger, Switzerland (BMW) 16
3 P.V.Harris, GB (BMW) 14

1961

125cc
1 T.Phillis, Australia (Honda) 48
2 E.Degner, E.Germany (MZ) 42
3 L.Taveri, Switzerland (Honda) 30

250cc
1 M.Hailwood, GB (Honda) 44
2 T.Phillis, Australia (Honda) 38
3 J.Redman, Rhodesia (Honda) 36

350cc
1 G.Hocking, Rhodesia (MV) 38
2 F.Stastny, Czechoslovakia (Jawa) 30
3 G.Havel, Czechoslovakia (Jawa) 19

500cc
1 G.Hocking, Rhodesia (MV) 48
2 M.Hailwood, GB (Norton/MV) 40
3 F.Perris, GB (Norton) 16

Sidecar
1 M.Deubel, W.Germany (BMW) 30
2 F.Scheidegger, Switzerland (BMW) 28
3 E.Strub, Switzerland (BMW) 14

1962

50cc
1 E.Degner, W.Germany (Suzuki) 41
2 H-G.Anscheidt, W.Ger. (Kreidler) 36
3 L.Taveri, Switzerland (Honda) 29

125cc
1 L.Taveri, Switzerland (Honda) 48
2 J.Redman, Rhodesia (Honda) 38
3 T.Robb, Ireland (Honda) 30

250cc
1 J.Redman, Rhodesia (Honda) 48
2 R.McIntyre, Scotland (Honda) 32
3 A.Wheeler, GB (Guzzi) 19

350cc
1 J.Redman, Rhodesia (Honda) 32
2 M.Hailwood, GB (MV) 20
3 T.Robb, Ireland (Honda) 18

500cc
1 M.Hailwood, GB (MV) 40
2 A.Shepherd, GB (Matchless) 29
3 P.Read, GB (Norton) 11

Sidecar
1 M.Deubel, W.Germany (BMW) 30
2 F.Camathias, Switzerland (BMW) 26
3 F.Scheidegger, Switzerland (BMW) 18

1963

50cc
1 H.Anderson, New Zealand (Suzuki) 34
2 H-G.Anscheidt, W.Ger. (Kreidler) 32
3 E.Degner, W.Germany (Suzuki) 30

125cc
1 H.Anderson, New Zealand (Suzuki) 54
2 L.Taveri, Switzerland (Honda) 38
3 J.Redman, Rhodesia (Honda) 35

250cc
1 J.Redman, Rhodesia (Honda) 44
2 T.Provini, Italy (Morini) 42
3 F.Ito, Japan (Yamaha) 26

350cc
1 J.Redman, Rhodesia (Honda) 32
2 M.Hailwood, GB (MV) 28
3 L.Taveri, Switzerland (Honda) 16

500cc
1 M.Hailwood, GB (MV) 40
2 A.Shepherd, GB (Matchless) 21
3 J.Hartle, GB (Gilera) 20

Sidecar
1 M.Deubel, W.Germany (BMW) 22
2 F.Camathias, Switzerland (BMW) 20
3 F.Scheidegger, Switzerland (BMW) 20

1964

50cc
1 H.Anderson, New Zealand (Suzuki) 38
2 R.Bryans, Ireland (Honda) 30
3 H-G.Anscheidt, W.Ger. (Kreidler) 29

125cc
1 L.Taveri, Switzerland (Honda) 46
2 J.Redman, Rhodesia (Honda) 36
3 H.Anderson, New Zealand (Suzuki) 34

250cc
1 P.Read, GB (Yamaha) 46
2 J.Redman, Rhodesia (Honda) 42
3 A.Shepherd, GB (MZ) 23

350cc
1 J.Redman, Rhodesia (Honda) 40
2 B.Beale, Rhodesia (Honda) 24
3 M.Duff, Canada (AJS) 20

500cc
1 M.Hailwood, GB (MV) 40
2 J.Ahearn, Australia (Norton) 25
3 P.Read, GB (Matchless) 25

Sidecar
1 M.Deubel, W.Germany (BMW) 28
2 F.Scheidegger, Switzerland (BMW) 26
3 C.Seeley, GB (BMW) 17

1965

50cc
1 R.Bryans, Ireland (Honda) 36
2 L.Taveri, Switzerland (Honda) 32
3 H.Anderson, New Zealand (Suzuki) 32

125cc
1 H.Anderson, New Zealand (Suzuki) 56
2 F.Perris, GB (Suzuki) 44
3 D.Woodman, GB (MZ) 28

250cc
1 P.Read, GB (Yamaha) 56
2 M.Duff, Canada (Yamaha) 42
3 J.Redman, Rhodesia (Honda) 34

350cc
1 J.Redman, Rhodesia (Honda) 38
2 G.Agostini, Italy (MV) 32
3 M.Hailwood, GB (MV) 20

500cc
1 M.Hailwood, GB (MV) 48
2 G.Agostini, Italy (MV) 38
3 P.Driver, South Africa (Matchless) 26

Sidecar
1 F.Scheidegger, Switzerland (BMW) 32
2 M.Deubel, W.Germany (BMW) 26
3 G.Auerbacher, W.Germany (BMW) 15

1966

50cc
1 H-G.Anscheidt, W.Germany (Suzuki) 28
2 R.Bryans, Ireland (Honda) 26
3 L.Taveri, Switzerland (Honda) 26

125cc
1 L.Taveri, Switzerland (Honda) 46
2 W.Ivy, GB (Yamaha) 40
3 R.Bryans, Ireland (Honda) 32

250cc
1 M.Hailwood, GB (Honda) 56
2 P.Read, GB (Yamaha) 34
3 J.Redman, Rhodesia (Honda) 20

350cc
1 M.Hailwood, GB (Honda) 48
2 G.Agostini, Italy (MV) 42
3 R.Pasolini, Italy (Aermacchi) 17

500cc
1 G.Agostini, Italy (MV) 36
2 M.Hailwood, GB (Honda) 30
3 J.Findlay, Australia (Matchless) 20

Sidecar
1 F.Scheidegger, Switzerland (BMW) 24
2 M.Deubel, W.Germany (BMW) 20
3 C.Seeley, GB (BMW) 13

1967

50cc
1 H-G.Anscheidt, W.Germany (Suzuki) 30
2 Y.Katayama, Japan (Suzuki) 28
3 S.Graham, GB (Suzuki) 22

125cc
1 W.Ivy, GB (Yamaha) 56
2 P.Read, GB (Yamaha) 40
3 S.Graham, GB (Suzuki) 38

250cc
1 M.Hailwood, GB (Honda) 50
2 P.Read, GB (Yamaha) 50
3 W.Ivy, GB (Yamaha) 46

350cc
1 M.Hailwood, GB (Honda) 40
2 G.Agostini, Italy (MV) 32
3 R.Bryans, Ireland (Honda) 20

500cc
1 G.Agostini, Italy (MV) 46
2 M.Hailwood, GB (Honda) 46
3 J.Hartle, GB (Matchless) 22

Sidecar
1 K.Enders, W.Germany (BMW) 40
2 G.Auerbacher, W.Germany (BMW) 32
3 S.Schauzu, W.Germany (BMW) 28

1968

50cc
1 H-G.Anscheidt, W.Germany (Suzuki) 24
2 P.Lodewijkx, Holland (Jamathi) 17
3 B.Smith, Australia (Derbi) 15

125cc
1 P.Read, GB (Yamaha) 40
2 W.Ivy, GB (Yamaha) 34
3 G.Molloy, New Zealand (Bultaco) 15

250cc
1 P.Read, GB (Yamaha) 52
2 W.Ivy, GB (Yamaha) 52
3 H.Rosner, E.Germany (MZ) 32

350cc
1 G.Agostini, Italy (MV) 32
2 R.Pasolini, Italy (Benelli) 18
3 K.Carruthers, Australia (Aermacchi) 17

500cc
1 G.Agostini, Italy (MV) 48
2 J.Findlay, Australia (Matchless) 34
3 G.Marsovszky, Switz. (Matchless) 10

Sidecar
1 H.Fath, W.Germany (Urs) 27
2 G.Auerbacher, W.Germany (BMW) 22
3 S.Schauzu, W.Germany (BMW) 19

1969

50cc
1 A.Nieto, Spain (Derbi) 76
2 A.Toersen, Holland (Kreidler) 75
3 B.Smith, Australia (Derbi) 69

125cc
1 D.Simmonds, GB (Kawasaki) 90
2 D.Braun, W.Germany (Suzuki) 59
3 C.van Dongen, Holland (Suzuki) 51

250cc
1 K.Carruthers, Australia (Benelli) 89
2 K.Andersson, Sweden (Yamaha) 84
3 S.Herrero, Spain (Ossa) 83

350cc
1 G.Agostini, Italy (MV) 90
2 S.Grassetti, Italy (Yamaha/Jawa) 47
3 G.Visenzi, Italy (Yamaha) 45

500cc
1 G.Agostini, Italy (MV) 105
2 G.Marsovszky, Switzerland (Linto) 47
3 G.Nash, GB (Norton) 45

Sidecar
1 K.Enders, W.Germany (BMW) 60
2 H.Fath, W.Germany (Urs) 55
3 G.Auerbacher, W.Germany 40

1970

50cc
1 A.Nieto, Spain (Derbi) 87
2 A.Toersen, Holland (Jamathi) 75
3 R.Kunz, W.Germany (Kreidler) 66

125cc
1 D.Braun, W.Germany (Suzuki) 84
2 A.Nieto, Spain (Derbi) 72
3 B.Jansson, Sweden (Maico) 62

250cc
1 R.Gould, GB (Yamaha) 102
2 K.Carruthers, Australia (Yamaha) 84
3 K.Andersson, Sweden (Yamaha) 67

350cc
1 G.Agostini, Italy (MV) 90
2 K.Carruthers, Aus. (Benelli/Yamaha) 58
3 R.Pasolini, Italy (Benelli) 46

500cc
1 G.Agostini, Italy (MV) 90
2 G.Molloy, New Zealand (Kawasaki) 62
3 A.Bergamonti, Italy (Aermacchi/MV) 59

Sidecar
1 K.Enders, W.Germany (BMW) 73
2 G.Auerbacher, W.Germany (BMW) 62
3 S.Schauzu, W.Germany (BMW) 56

1971

50cc
1 J.de Vries, Holland (Kreidler) 75
2 A.Nieto, Spain (Derbi) 69
3 J.Schurgers, Holland (Kreidler) 42

125cc
1 A.Nieto, Spain (Derbi) 87
2 B.Sheene, GB (Suzuki) 79
3 B.Jansson, Sweden (Maico) 64

250cc
1 P.Read, GB (Yamaha) 73
2 R.Gould, GB (Yamaha) 68
3 J.Saarinen, Finland (Yamaha) 64

350cc
1 G.Agostini, Italy (MV) 90
2 J.Saarinen, Finland (Yamaha) 63
3 K-I.Carlsson, Sweden (Yamaha) 39

500cc
1 G.Agostini, Italy (MV) 90
2 K.Turner, New Zealand (Suzuki) 58
3 R.Bron, Holland (Suzuki) 57

Sidecar
1 H.Owesle, W.Germany (Munch) 69
2 A.Butscher, W.Germany (BMW) 57
3 S.Schauzu, W.Germany (BMW) 57

1972

50cc
1 A.Nieto, Spain (Derbi) 69
2 J.de Vries, Holland (Kreidler) 69
3 T.Timmer, Holland (Jamathi) 50

125cc
1 A.Nieto, Spain (Derbi) 97
2 K.Andersson, Sweden (Yamaha) 87
3 C.Mortimer, GB (Yamaha) 87

250cc
1 J.Saarinen, Finland (Yamaha) 94
2 R.Pasolini, Italy (Aermacchi) 93
3 R.Gould, GB (Yamaha) 88

350cc
1 G.Agostini, Italy (MV) 102
2 J.Saarinen, Finland (Yamaha) 89
3 R.Pasolini, Italy (Aermacchi) 78

500cc
1 G.Agostini, Italy (MV) 105
2 A.Pagani, Italy (MV) 87
3 B.Kneubuhler, Switz. (Yamaha) 57

Sidecar
1 K.Enders, W.Germany (BMW) 72
2 H.Luthringshauser, W.Ger. (BMW) 63
3 S.Schauzu, W.Germany (BMW) 62

THE AMERICAN SCENE

Undoubtedly the most significant development in motorcycle sport in the early 1970s was the progress that road racing made in the United States, and the effects that this had on European racing. The American motor cycling governing

body had fallen out with the European authorities in the early 1920s, when they felt that the interests of motor cycling would be better served by restricting the bikes used in competition to basically sports machines.

Incredibly fast pit stops are part of the American scene. Here Triumph teamster Don Castro takes on five gallons of fuel in six seconds by using an aircraft style refuelling system. On the left a helper stands by with a fire-extinguisher – a necessary precaution because engines are kept running.

Californian Don Emde in victory lane at Daytona after winning the 1972 Daytona '200' on a Yamaha. With him are his mother and sister (*left*) and his father Floyd who won the same race on an Indian in 1948.

The Europeans did not agree and any FICM licensed rider who competed in an American Motorcycle Association event risked suspension. Few did – or wanted too. For until the late 1960s there was little road racing in America. Even the famous Daytona 200, now recognised as one of the most important road races in the world, was run on a circuit that was half sand and half road until 1961, when it switched to the then new Daytona International Speedway.

Another deterrent was the AMA insistence on sports-based racing machines, for this meant that most of the bikes used in European grand prix racing were not eligible for the few AMA road races. In the immediate post-war years the single overhead camshaft Manx Norton was allowed and, prepared by British tuners Francis Beart and Steve Lancefield, proved very successful on the original beach-road circuit at Daytona, winning four years in succession (1949–52). But the double overhead camshaft 'Featherbed' model was outlawed by the AMA.

In America the sport developed on lines well removed from the mainstream. The AMA championship series embraced several different types of racing, including half-mile and mile dirt tracks (mainly run on loose surfaced horse racing ovals), road racing and American-style TT racing (this is a cross between dirt track racing and moto cross, and events are run on short graded courses that include one scrambles-style jump).

At the same time the AMA took far more interest in the financial side of things than their European counterparts. They insisted on race promoters paying reasonable prize money and the number of championship points at stake at a championship meeting are in direct ratio to the prize fund. This is a simple but very effective method of rewarding the big-money events by automatically up-grading their status in the eyes of the riders and ensuring that all the top-liners attend – money plus more points than can be gained at lesser meetings proving a powerful attraction.

In Europe the FIM buried their heads in the sand when it came to money. They insisted that finance was a matter to be thrashed out between the organisers and the riders. This policy was not surprising because the FIM is largely made up of organisers or of people with close connections with promoters. In contrast the AMA is far more closely allied to the motor-cycle dealers and to the manufacturers. The FIM's attitude led to steadily falling incomes for the riders as individual organisers cut the money they paid – both starting money (the amount paid to a rider provided that he qualifies and starts in a race) and prize funds.

With prices increasing as inflation swept across Europe in the early 1970s and with the cost of racing machines and their spares rocketing as more sophisticated bikes became available this led inevitably to a crisis. Competitors simply could not make racing pay. At last the FIM did act and in 1972 a 'working party' of members of the FIM's Commission Sportive (CSI) was appointed to look into the whole question of grand prix finance.

The sport in America also developed on different lines when it came to capacity classes. In the 1930s the AMA agreed that overhead valve and single overhead camshaft engines up to 500cc should race on equal terms with the 750cc side-valve vee-twins then popular with the two American companies racing, Harley-Davidson and Indian.

Unlike Europeans they were content with a single big machine class, but as lightweights became popular a 250cc class was added in the 1960s. There had been half-hearted attempts to bring the AMA back into the FIM fold before but it was not until late in the decade, when America was in the grip of a fantastic motor cycling boom, that any real progress was made. Then enlightened men on both sides of the Atlantic recognised the advantages of putting motor-cycle sport on a really world-wide basis and the AMA was re-admitted to the FIM.

This was an opportune moment. The trend towards 750cc 'Superbikes' was well established and coinciding with the news that America was back in the FIM came the AMA's decision to lift the capacity limit for their big bike class to 750cc for all types of engines. This delighted the manufacturers and the race at Daytona in March 1970 ushered in a new era of road racing. For the first time top class European road racers met the ace Americans on level terms – and the works teams, that had faded from the European scene, were back in force.

And so was Mike Hailwood! Since 1969 he had been restricting his motor-cycle racing to occasional outings on borrowed machines, slotted

Action at Daytona as the first wave of starters heads for the banking during the 1970 race. Dick Mann (Honda) leads and although he was caught and passed he fought back to win the race. He won again in 1971 on a BSA.

Mike Hailwood's last big motorcycle race was at Daytona in 1971 when he rode a three-cylinder 750cc BSA for the British factory. Despite crashing at 150mph in practice when the power of a new double disc brake set-up caught him out, Hailwood fought for the lead until the BSA failed.

Above: Mike Hailwood (BSA) leads the 1970 Daytona '200' from Gary Nixon (Triumph) and Dick Mann (Honda). Behind them Kel Carruthers (Yamaha, 75).

in between car racing engagements and mainly done to oblige promotors and to earn money – his appearance on a bike cost the organisers at least £1,000 and probably added 5,000 to the gate. At Daytona he joined the new BSA squad, teaming with Americans Jim Rice and Dave Aldana.

Riding the similar 750cc three-cylinder Triumphs were American Gary Nixon, who had twice won the AMA championship for Triumph, using their twin-cylinder 500cc machines, Gene Romero, Don Castro and Triumph tester Percy Tait. Honda fielded four factory-backed four-cylinder CR750 models with their number one machine ridden by veteran American all-rounder Dick Mann and prepared by Bob Hansen. Suzuki had a team of twin-cylinder 500cc racers and Yamaha and Harley-Davidson were there too.

In the race the BSA-Triumph team set the pace but overheating problems put their leading machines out and Mann was the winner on the only factory Honda to last the distance, the wily American pulling a big gear and keeping the revs down – a lesson he had learned through competing

regularly in the Florida classic. Romero took second place – and went on to win the AMA championship for Triumph.

For 1971 Kawasaki joined in with a racing version of their 500cc three-cylinder two-stroke but this did not stop Mann from winning at Daytona again. This time he was on a BSA 'three' and again he outlasted his rivals, Hailwood and then Paul Smart (Triumph), both of whom retired with mechanical troubles. Dick Mann finished the year as AMA champion.

The booming scene in America contrasted with the hard times that the European riders were going through – despite the fact that crowds were up (often four or five times as many as watched a big event in the States). Inevitably some top liners were attracted to ride for the American-based teams. Kel Carruthers, 250cc world champion in

Above: Cal Rayborn (Harley-Davidson) leads Ray Pickrell (Triumph) during the 1972 Anglo-American match race series. They shared the honours, each winning three races.
Left: Hailwood (*left*) and Gary Nixon, top European and American riders of their era.

1969, joined the Yamaha team and for 1972 Paul Smart, left without factory support when the Triumph racing department folded, accepted an offer to ride a Kawasaki for the factory-backed Team Hansen.

But there were benefits for Europe. Most of the machines developed for American racing were suitable for grand prix racing (notably the 250cc and 350cc Yamahas, the 500cc Kawasaki and the 500cc Suzuki). And early in 1971 a common set of regulations for the big machines (dubbed Formula 750) was drawn up when officials of the British Auto-Cycle Union met AMA delegates in America; the FIM adopted this class internationally within a few months.

The colourful scene at Daytona
Top, left: Dave Aldana (BSA).
Top, right: race flags.
Middle, left: 1970 American champion
Gene Romero.
Centre: Harley Davidson team at Daytona
1970 with Mark Brelsford, 1972 American
champion, waving.
Right: Mert Lawwill, 1969 American champion
with his works Harley-Davidson.
Bottom, left: Walt Fulton (Kawasaki).
Bottom, centre: Gary Nixon with a 1972
Kawasaki.
Bottom, right: George Kerker (Norton).

The cause of bike racing was further developed by the Anglo-American Match Race series. This was first held in England in 1971 when it was sponsored by the BSA-Triumph group. That year it was, naturally enough, confined to BSA-Triumph works riders (five from each country) and was won by the British team. In 1972 it was open to any make of machine and Cal Rayborn (Harley-Davidson) proved that American racers are just as good as British by winning three of the six races. Despite his efforts the British team won again.

Now the FIM have agreed that the Formula 750 class shall have championship status. It will be interesting to see if it succeeds in bringing the factory teams back into European racing. . . .

Above, left to right: embarrassing moment for Ireland's Ralph Bryans at Daytona in 1970! In the first shot he has just been flipped off his factory 750cc Honda as the rear wheel came round under heavy acceleration – bike and rider are travelling right to left at about 70 mph . . . Bryans and Honda slide along the banking . . . Bryans jumps up and heads for the safety of the infield . . . as other riders roar past the Honda catches fire. Bryans stands by.

Below, left to right: hectic start to the 1972 Daytona '200'. Jerry Christopher has come off his Kawasaki at 100 mph as the field brakes for the infield turn. That's Jerry on the left standing on his head! . . . braking to avoid the melee Ralph White (Yamaha, 15) crashes too. Canadian Duane McDaniels (Yamaha, 27) takes to the grass but American champion Dick Mann (BSA, 1) just gets through the gap as the bikes slide off the track and on to the grass . . . Ralph White is still bouncing as Christopher's Kawasaki somersaults across the grass behind McDaniels . . . officials run to pick up the pieces. No riders were seriously hurt in this incident.

Following pages:
Top, left: Jack Findlay (Jada) and Charlie Sanby (Suzuki) get away at the start of the 1972 Senior TT.
Middle, left: Dick Mann (BSA), Daytona 1972.
Bottom, left: Gary Nixon (Kawasaki), Daytona 1972.
Top, centre: Agostini and Pagani on the winner's rostrum at the Dutch TT 1972.
Bottom, centre: end of the 1972 Daytona '200'.
Top, right: Dave Smith (Yamaha) looks for Kenny Roberts (Yamaha) at Daytona 1972.
Middle, right: Ron Grant (Suzuki 750 cc) at Daytona 1972.
Bottom, right: Kenny Roberts (Yamaha), Daytona 1972.

INDEX